Christmas 1994

To /

+

Robert, Ann, +

Michael D.

BASIC
GOLFING
TECHNIQUES

EDITED BY
SEAN CALLERY

NEW
BURLINGTON
BOOKS

A QUINTET BOOK

First published in 1991 by
New Burlington Books
6 Blundell Street
London N7 9BH

Exclusive to Coles in Canada

ISBN 1-85348-330-3

This book was designed and produced by
Quintet Publishing Limited
6 Blundell Street
London N7 9BH

Creative Director: Peter Bridgewater
Art Director/Designer: Terry Jeavons
Project Editor: Sean Callery

Typeset in Great Britain by
Central Southern Typesetters, Eastbourne
Manufactured in Hong Kong by
Regent Publishing Services Limited
Printed in Hong Kong by
Leefung-Asco Printers Limited

The material in this publication previously
appeared in *Golf School, Golfing School* and
Beginners Guide to Golf

CONTENTS

INTRODUCTION

Many golfers play just for fun, highlighting the obvious benefits of companionship, friendly rivalry and exercise, as well as a solution to filling in some of those hours of leisure. Here, in particular, golf has much to offer since it enables people of varying ability to play together and compete on level terms.

The dangers of playing golf at this level, however, are all too obvious. Because it is possible as a high-handicap golfer to play against those of a much higher standard and compete at club level, the incentives to improve may not be as strong as they could be.

In this respect golf is no different to any other sport, where the object is always to play better and compete harder. This, after all, is the instinctive way of enjoying the game – and this should always be encouraged as a healthy motivation. For the average player, there is bound to be a limit to the improvement that can be achieved. No one is suggesting that in time everyone who takes up golf seriously should become a scratch player. But the target all players should set themselves is to aim to bring that handicap down and strive for their own personal level of achievement.

GETTING PRIORITIES RIGHT

If you want to get the most from your golf, you should never be satisfied by being mediocre all the time. There is nothing easier than playing your way around the course, rejoicing over a few lucky shots but accepting that most were inevitably modest and quite often bad. If you were honest with yourself, you can never really claim to have enjoyed the round. But worse than this, there will be times when the effect is positively destructive. Having sliced the ball into the rough or chipped short of the green into yet another bunker for the umpteenth time, you will quickly lose heart and your game will deteriorate even further.

Only the best players can expect to get it right most of the time, and rest assured even the top professionals cannot guarantee every shot they play. What they *have* learned, however, is to know what they should be doing and, when things do not work out as planned, where they are going wrong – this should be every golfer's objective.

There are many qualities that go to making a good golfer. Ability is the most obvious one, but there are others that, even without too much ability, could be developed to help you with your game. Of these, fitness is one of the most important not least because it is closely linked to concentration. The overall approach to the game in general, and each shot in particular, is one area that every would-be golfer should work hard at. This is why the mental aspects are so vital – thinking carefully about each shot, which club to use, where to play the ball, what the state of the ground is. You need plenty of patience when the ball just will not run for you and plenty of finesse when it comes to the awkward or delicate shot. Timing is critical, and a good sense of this is a major step toward mastery of the required techniques.

Less important, possibly, but equally a useful asset, is strength. Power in the shot is determined more by the quality of execution, including the timing, than physical strength. There will be times when shot selection may be determined by the physique and power of the player. Any advantages, however, tend to balance themselves out over the course of a round and do not handicap the weaker player to any extent.

LEARNING THE BASICS

You may be surprised to hear that golf is essentially a simple game. The better the player, the more the basic elements of golf can be developed; but this takes time and a great deal of practice. For the average player – and particularly for the beginner – the golden rule is *keep it simple*.

The vast majority of the problems experienced by the average golfer are self-inflicted. It is vital that you understand from the very beginning that bad habits are easy to develop and very difficult to get out of. The obvious solution is to avoid getting into them, so always go back to the basics when you find yourself in trouble. If you have learned these thoroughly you will find that most of your problems can be solved by concentrating on executing the basic techniques correctly.

Why are these basic techniques so vital to the game of golf? Because they concern all the elements of preparation for the shot, since virtually all the faults in the shots you play can be traced back to the stages prior to the strike. These include the setting-up procedure, the grip on the club and the development of the swing. Understanding these and practising the right techniques will go a long way to making you a reasonable player.

As with any ball game, control is the key factor. In the case of golf, this means knowing in which direction the ball will travel, what kind of flight-path it will have and how far it will go. Often average club players sacrifice control because elements of their basic technique have gone wrong. If these techniques are not learned and practised thoroughly, there is no way of tracing the cause of the problem or putting it right. In this situation every shot becomes a matter of guess-work and luck plays an ever-increasing role in where the ball goes.

Pool and tennis are good examples of this principle. In pool you must first learn the right cue action and how to hit the ball straight before you can hope to master the angled shot or put spin on the cue ball. The same is true for tennis. Until you have complete control over your racket and can play a clean forehand or backhand drive, you are wasting your time attempting the more complex volley or smash shots.

Your approach to golf should be exactly the same. Any attempt to play a delicate shot with a lofted iron or to control a hook shot around an obstacle that lies ahead of you will invariably end in failure if you cannot drive the ball reasonably straight with your standard shots, using irons and woods. The message is clear and obvious – *do not run before you can walk.* The more you concentrate on, and the better you perfect, the basic techniques, the easier and more successful the harder shots will be.

VARYING YOUR GAME

One of the great joys of golf is the enormous variety of courses on which it can be played. Wherever you go, you are guaranteed a different set of holes, each with their own special characteristics and individual problems. Add to this the fact that the way any course plays will depend on the prevailing conditions at the time and you will quickly realize that golf offers a new challenge virtually every time you step onto a course, even when your golf is played over the same course.

Despite the many variables you will be confronted with, there are certain characteristics that typify particular courses and thus divide them into two basic categories – links and inland.

Links courses are among the oldest in the world and are regarded by some as the more traditional venue for golf. The British Open championship is always played on a links course. Links courses are strongly associated with Scotland, where arguably the game of golf as we know it was born. The game's governing body presides at the Royal and Ancient Golf Club at St Andrews in Fife, Scotland.

Links courses provide the greatest challenge to the golfer because they are natural strips of land bordering the sea and are consequently exposed to all the elements. The ground is often sandy and the turf short and coarse, so the lie of the ball is usually very tight. Coastal vegetation in the form of gorse and heather can pose a real threat to the wayward golfer who misses the fairway. In addition, the greens on this type of course are generally very fast and often undulating.

Inland courses, on the other hand, present a different challenge. Since they are purpose built, with specially designed man-made hazards, the contest is more one of golfer versus course architect. The grass is generally richer and softer and the often uniformly flat greens on the whole slower, making the outcome of pitch shots more predictable. The skill needed is not so much to cope with the elements as to avoid the problems awaiting the unsuspecting player in the form of bunkers and ponds, as well as trees and bushes on and around the fairway.

In both cases, playing can be a memorable experience. On the links courses the marine views are interesting and at times rugged and spectacular, while inland the richness and grandeur of the scenery cannot fail to impress. Naturally your mind should be concentrating on the shot in hand, but when that does go astray there is always some compensation to be had in admiring the surrounding scenery.

KEEPING IN PRACTICE

It is a mistake to think that simply playing a round or two of golf regularly will automatically improve your game. More often than not it will only perpetuate any faults you have developed until they eventually become a permanent feature of your game. You should remember that once on the course you must pay due consideration to other golfers waiting to play their round. Do not waste time by practising a particular shot or, which is just as bad, stand around discussing it afterwards.

The time to practice is between rounds, and it is very important that you approach this with a positive attitude. There is little point in swinging away aimlessly for hours on end. Concentrate on a particular technical aspect – whether it be your stance or a part of your swing – or the use of a particular club. A half-hour's serious practice is worth a great deal more than hours of unco-ordinated slogging, for not only does the practice have no purpose, but tired limbs will only aggravate the situation and do more harm than good to your golf.

Even with short periods of practice you can easily become bored, so set yourself targets and vary these to provide a constant challenge. You can make your life a lot easier – and the practice more effective – if you select the ground carefully. There is no point in playing off a bad lie if you want to develop a sound swing and hit the ball straight. Deliberately practising awkward shots is, of course, another matter.

One very important aspect of practising to eliminate faults is to seek the advice of a club teaching professional. Very often you may not be in a position – or have the experience – to identify exactly where you are going wrong. Then is the time to speak to an expert, so that you can be put right at an early stage. This does not mean that your tutor has to stand over you. If you take regular tuition, once he is familiar with your swing, a few words of advice may be all that is required to clarify a particular point or iron out a nagging problem.

GETTING STARTED

The road to mastering the basic technique of golf or improving your existing game is not an easy one. Only you can decide how seriously you wish to be a better golfer. The guidelines laid down in this book have been arranged to lead you through the essential stages of the game, and it cannot be stressed too strongly that the order of priorities is crucial if progress is to be made.

You may feel that your basic game is quite satisfactory, but that you want to improve on your spin shots or your play from bunkers. Before you rush to those particular sections, spend some time running through the basic techniques. It could just be that your swing is not quite as perfect as it should be and does not provide you with any sound foundation from which to adapt for specialist shots. And that might well be the answer to the problems you are having with spin shots or your bunker play.

Particularly for those starting from scratch, do not be in too much of a hurry to get out on the course. The more time you spend developing your technique, the better the results when you do go out for a round and the better equipped you will be to cope with the inevitable crises you find yourself in.

Finally, a word to all left-handed players. To simplify the instructions in this book, the various techniques have been discussed and illustrated as for right-handed golfers. Left-handed players should simply reverse these instructions where appropriate.

EQUIPMENT

Golf, and the equipment used to play it, have changed out of all recognition since the birth of the game. The days of playing with little more than wooden sticks have given way to current demands for equipment built to complex technical specifications. The development of equipment has matched the changes in the game and in the courses.

In the early days, when golfers used clubs with hickory shafts, their swings had to suit the characteristics of the shaft. The hickory shaft had torque, or twist, giving a natural turning in the shaft. Yesterday's golfer did not work against this, but turned it to his advantage. His swing plane was flatter, with a lot more hand and arm action. Opening up the club-face on the way back, he then brought it square to the ball and closed it on the way through. This meant the player had to aim to the right to allow for the draw that this swing had fashioned. This gave the shot over-spin, or top-spin, and so the run factor was very important. Neither fairways nor greens were watered, so golf courses suited the type of game where the object was to make the ball run after pitching.

With the introduction of steel shafts without torque, the golf swing had to change to suit the clubs and the modern square-to-square method came into favour. It eliminated the opening and closing of the club-face.

This coincided with the change in golf course practice. Watered greens came first, soon to be followed by watered fairways. Golf balls do not run as far on lush grass, so the swing concept changed, to provide height and flight.

When choosing equipment, you may start to play golf with a single club, a half-set or a full set, with new or used clubs. Many beginners buy a single used iron to begin with.

If you begin with just one new club, buy it from a source – a professional or sports shop – which can supply matching clubs singly. You can build up your set as your needs grow.

If you decide on a half-set, bear in mind that you may not be able to add matching clubs at a later date. Manufacturers often change models.

The third option is to buy a full set, new or used, straight away. A full set contains a maximum of 14 clubs. It usually consists of nine irons, four woods and a putter. Make sure, when choosing a full set, that the irons all match. Mixed irons do not constitute a set.

THE PUTTER

Many golfers think that a putter has no loft, but it actually has between two and four degrees. When struck with a putter, the ball skids for the first 20 per cent of its journey and then rolls, with over-spin, the remaining 80 per cent.

Putters come in many shapes and sizes. Whatever the design of the putter you must strike the ball consistently out of the 'sweet spot'. Many putters have lines or spots to help with the lining up, and players assume that this must be the sweet spot, but this is not always correct. To find the sweet spot, most professionals hold the putter loosely between the forefinger and thumb, allowing it to hang. Then, using one of those pencils with an eraser on the end, they tap the club-face with the eraser until they find the place which feels the most solid. This place is the sweet spot.

A ball not struck with the sweet spot of the putter will lose distance. That happens to any ball struck with either the toe or heel of the putter.

When putting, the putter should be grounded with the sweet spot directly behind the ball.

The lengths of putter shafts vary between 33 and 36 in (84 and 91 cm). The shafts are usually stiff. The weights vary between 15 and 18 oz (425 and 510 g).

Your choice of putter should be influenced by the speed of the greens at the course where you intend to play most of your golf. If they are fast, choose a lightweight putter: the slower the surface, the heavier the putter should be.

ABOVE: *To find the sweet spot of a putter, hold the putter loosely between the forefinger and thumb, allowing it to hang vertically. Using a pencil with an eraser on the end, tap the club-face with the eraser until you find the place which feels most solid. This is the sweet spot.*

RIGHT: *A set of irons consists of nine clubs. A half set is either the four even, or the five odd numbers, plus a wood and a putter.*

TOP: *When you buy a full set, make sure all the irons are by the same manufacturer and of the same model.*

RIGHT: *The loft on the clubs decreases as their numbers decrease.*

IRONS

There are two different ways of manufacturing iron heads for golf clubs: casting and forging.

The method for cast heads allows mass production of even complicated designs and ensures consistency of weight in each club-head. It also means that the lofts of each set will be perfectly matched. The materials used are of hard steel, and the production methods therefore make it difficult to manufacture heads to suit players who are not of standard height and build.

Forged heads are made from softer metals. Their softness means that they can be custom-ground and shaped to suit individuals. For this reason, most touring professionals choose to play with this type of club.

CLUB-HEAD

The long irons used for distance have the smallest numbers of the clubs in the set. The chipping, pitching and sand irons have the highest numbers. All share built-in design factors allowing the golfer to meet his individual needs. Golf club-heads come in different shapes to do different things. You must decide what you want your golf club to do. The centre of gravity and the lie of the club-head are the important features to examine when choosing clubs to suit your physique.

The centre of gravity relates to the distribution of the weight in the club-head. If you have trouble getting the ball into the air, you must select a club with the weight at the bottom of the club-head. When striking the ball, the centre of gravity

The rules of golf are codified and approved by the Royal and Ancient Golf Club of St Andrews and the United States Golf Association. The rules were last overhauled (and simplified) in 1984. You should find little difficulty in learning the basics very quickly, and should carry the rule-book out on the course for reference.

If you consider for a moment the potential complexity of rule-making for the game of golf – what may be hair, for example, when you are faced with an impossible lie, or what happens if your ball goes out of bounds – then you will realise that the rule-book is really a surprisingly short and succinct document.

will be below the centre of the ball, helping to lift it in the air, and resulting in a soaring flight.

On the other hand, many golfers feel that they hit the ball too high, and they must therefore select a club design where the weight has been positioned higher in the club-head. When striking the ball, the centre of gravity will be above the centre of the ball. This will help to keep the ball lower in flight. If the centre of gravity lies in the middle of the blade – behind the ball – then mid-flight will be achieved.

The lie of the club-head is the angle formed by a line through the centre of the shaft and the ground, when the club-head is placed flat in the address position.

An upright lie is favoured by taller golfers because their hands are farther from the ground.

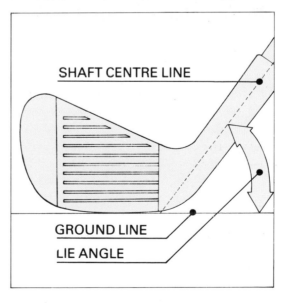

SHAFT CENTRE LINE

GROUND LINE

LIE ANGLE

LEFT: *The lie angle of the club-head is extremely important and is dependent upon the angle of the swing.*

The flatter lies put you slightly farther from the ball in the address position and are therefore more suited to the shorter golfer. If you take a club with too upright a lie for you, the heel of the club-head will be on the ground but the toe raised off it a little. When swinging into the ball with too upright a lie, the heel will hit the ground before the ball is sent away and the 'free' toe will come round, closing the club-face and sending the ball, for a right-hander, to the left. If the lie is too flat, the opposite will happen. At the address the toe will be on the ground but the heel will be clear of it. When striking into the shot, the toe will hit the ground, spinning the heel past the toe and opening the club-face, shooting the ball to the right.

CLUB DESIGN AND NUMBERS (RULE 4)

All clubs you are likely to come across will of course comply with the rules, any manufacturer who is unsure about the legality of a new design must submit a prototype to St Andrews for a ruling. The ruling on the number of clubs allowed is more important for the beginner; you can play with a maximum of 14 clubs, and cannot replace a damaged club or add to your set, once you start to play, by borrowing from another player who is playing out on the course.

IRONS			
Iron NUMBER	**Strong loft** DEGREES	**Standard loft** DEGREES	**Weak loft** DEGREES
3	22	24	26
4	26	28	30
5	30	32	34
6	34	36	38
7	38	40	42
8	42	44	46
9	46	48	50
Pitching wedge	50	52	54
Sand wedge	54	56	58

Spend some time and seek professional advice over obtaining clubs. They should suit you for length, lie, swing weight and centre of gravity. Between each number in a set of irons, there are four degrees of loft, representing 10–12 yd (9–11 m) of flight.

The weight of each iron club increases throughout the set. In an average set, the lightest is the 3-iron at 15 oz (425 g) and each succeeding iron gets heavier, with the 9-iron weighing 16 oz (454 g). The sand wedge and pitching wedge are designed to be even heavier for their particular roles.

WOODS

There is no end to the selection of drivers and fairway clubs coming onto the golfers' market, with new designs of heads, and variations in weight displacement and shaft tensions. They are all still generally referred to as woods, although many clubs now attracting increasing support are metal-headed. These are hollow and the design places the weight around the perimeter of the head. This helps the golfer to achieve consistency in his shots, even when he fails to strike the ball in the middle of the club-face. He also finds help from the lower centre of gravity of the club-head, as opposed to the wooden club-head. This sends the ball higher and makes the club easier to use. Many professionals are switching to metal. A wider selection of lofts is now available for metal-headed clubs.

The heads of wooden clubs are still either persimmon or laminated maple. Persimmon is thought, quite wrongly, to be the harder of the

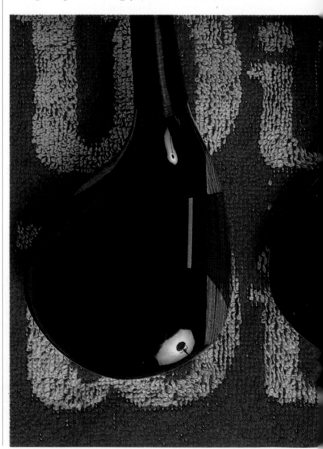

two. Laminated maple has an advantage over persimmon, in that a matched set of laminated woods – a driver, a 3-wood and a 5-wood – have a greater consistency of weight. Irons should, as was emphasized, be bought in a set, but this is not a must for the woods. It is acceptable to find three unmatched clubs to do the jobs required: a driver to hit off the tee, a fairway wood to play long shots and a more lofted club for the intermediate shots.

A good quality set of headcovers should always be placed on these clubs to protect them from being marked by the heads of the irons when they are taken out of the bag and replaced. When the headcovers get wet, take them off after the round of golf and dry them. Leaving them wet on your clubs will cause gradual but severe deterioration in the club-head. It can cause rust on metal heads. On persimmon, it can cause the wood to swell and with the laminated clubs the polyurethane coating is attacked, ultimately causing the thinning paint to chip.

WOODS			
Wood NUMBER	**Strong loft** DEGREES	**Standard loft** DEGREES	**Weak loft** DEGREES
1	10	11	12
2	12	13	14
3	15	16	17
4	18	19	20
5	21	22	23

LEFT AND BELOW: *A set of woods can consist of three or four clubs. Most modern sets have only three: the driver and the three and five woods. The driver has the biggest head and the deepest face. The club-heads become smaller as their loft increases, which gives the five wood club-head a lower centre of gravity.*

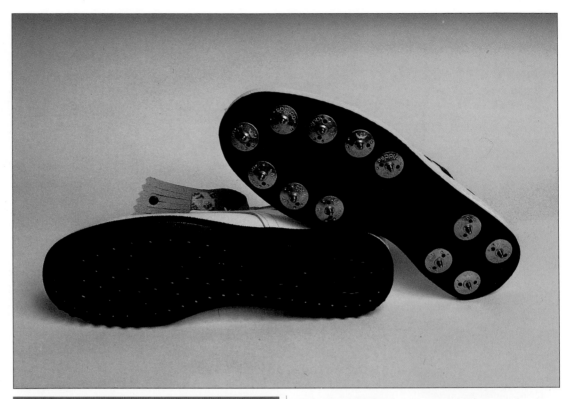

SHOES

Golf professionals' shops are usually stocked with a wide choice of golf shoes in various colours. This market is highly competitive, with Far Eastern countries claiming a share. Your priority is to seek comfort. You walk a long way on a golf course (especially if you do not keep to the fairway), you climb and you descend, you stride out and you wait about. A comfortable pair of golf shoes are two good companions you should choose to take with you.

Should you buy spiked or non-spiked golf shoes? The weight of spikes makes these shoes heavier to wear. Spikes give a slightly better grip to the ground and are helpful when walking on hilly courses, but on hard fairways where they do not fully bite, they lose their advantage over the non-spiked and ligher shoe. Take care not to damage the green when wearing spikes.

The choice of shoes now available to golfers dazzles the customers. Should you buy leather or non-leather uppers, with leather or non-leather soles? Comfort is the deciding factor, plus, of course, how much you can afford to pay for it.

ABOVE: *Golf shoe spikes are not of course as sharp as those of an athlete's shoe. They are made of stainless steel and should not deteriorate.*

RIGHT: *The ball has a solid centre core made of moulded rubber, covered with a pigmented Surlyn cover.*

GOLF BALLS

The game of golf has evolved around the little white ball. This book is about hitting it correctly. Take away some of the golf clubs and you still have a game. Take away the ball and you are left with practice swings. The pursuit of this ball on courses across the world has provided pleasure and despair, has led to new industries manufacturing clubs and equipment, has created thousands of jobs, has made millionaires of top players and has led to improvements in its own manufacture.

Briefly, there are three separate types of golf ball: solid, three-piece and two-piece. The solid ball is at the bottom end of the market and is favoured by many beginners, mainly because of its low price. Older golfers may remember taking golf balls to pieces, peeling off the outer covers so that they could unravel miles of rubber bands wound round the soft centre of the ball. This type of ball is still manufactured today, although its components and Balata cover have been improved by modern technology. It is known as the three-piece ball.

New technology has also given birth to the two-piece ball, which has a harder feel in its blended Surlyn cover, and is a lot less likely to be damaged by mis-hit shots. Inside the two-piece is a resilient core of blended resins.

There are two sizes of golf balls, the 1.62 and the 1.68. The numbers refer to the diameter in inches. The traditional golf ball is the 1.62 as approved by the Royal and Ancient Golf Club of St Andrews, the ruling body of golf. From America came the slightly larger 1.68. This size has now won international approval and is the only one permitted in national and international competitions. Golf ball manufacturers still produce the 1.62, but in decreasing numbers.

ABOVE: *Stages of the Balata ball manufacture: the rubber centre is filled with water. Rubber bands are wound round it. The Balata outer cup has the dimples moulded in, painted, lacquered and stamped 'Titleist'.*

LEFT: *Manufacture of the Surlyn covered ball: in the US this ball is called the 'Titleist D T' and in the UK, the 'Titleist 384 pts'. The solid rubber centre has rubber bands wound around it. It is then given the Surlyn cup, which is not painted but pigmented.*

ABOVE: *Always place your marker behind the ball in direct line with the hole.*

ABOVE: *Clearly, a pitch mark like this spoils the putting surface for everyone else.*

ABOVE: *Lift up the impacted turf and tap the area flat with the sole of your putter.*

GOLF BAGS

To carry or to trolley – that is the question. The best carry bags are collapsible and therefore have no supports, but a trolley bag needs some side supports to keep it firm on the trolley. When buying a carry bag lightness is the important factor. It is a long way round a golf course and, when full of the other accessories as well as the clubs, the bag is carrying quite a heavy load. A trolley bag on the other hand can be a little larger. The small amount of extra weight when placed on a trolley will not be noticed.

Many players judge a bag by how big or wide the top is. That is only half the story. The bottom is as important, if not more so. If it is too small, then the grips get jammed together and rub against each other when they are pulled out. When watching the touring professionals, weekend golfers look at the size of their golf bags and think how uncomfortable it must be for their caddies to carry them around. In fact they are well designed so that the weight is distributed evenly over the whole bag.

Whether you carry or trolley depends ultimately on your fitness and your pocket.

TROLLEYS

It is a false economy to choose a trolley from the cheap range. The difference in design is usually considerable, while the difference in price is much less. Choose a trolley which you can pull standing upright.

MISCELLANEOUS ITEMS

Other useful items you will require on your round include the following:

Umbrella: Be prepared for that shower which hits you on the hole furthest from the clubhouse. Remember, you may not seek shelter when playing in a competition.

Tee pegs: Both wooden and plastic pegs are available. The wooden pegs are favoured by those golfers who dislike the plastic pegs sometimes marking the faces of their woods. However they break more easily than the plastic pegs, which are cheaper and more popular.

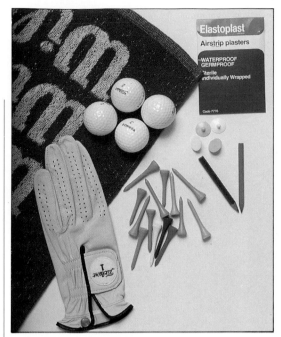

LEFT: Important items needed when you go onto the course: a left hand glove to help give you added strength and adhesion in your grip: tee-pegs, marker, pencils, golf balls, and adhesive tape.

OPPOSITE: Equipment you will need before you begin to play a round of golf. All are necessary and of equal importance to your success.

Ball markers: Markers are small discs which are used to mark the position of the ball on the green when you have picked it up for cleaning, or because it is impeding the shots of others. They are a must for the golf bag, or better still, a handy pocket.

There is only one correct way to use a marker. Stand behind the ball facing the hole. Place the marker behind and underneath the ball, making sure that you do not touch the ball. Never place a marker in front of the ball, or at the side of it, because there is a risk that, with loss of concentration when studying the next putt, you could place the ball back in front of the marker.

Pitchfork: A pocket pitchfork is carried by all golfers who extend courtesy to other players. A constant complaint in the locker room is aimed at golfers who have not repaired their pitch marks on the green. The ball dropping down into a soft green from its high arc makes an indentation on the putting surface. It is every golfer's duty to repair his own pitch mark.

Pencil: Similarly, you need a scorecard bearing all the local rules, including information on those holes of the course at which shots may be claimed when playing a match.

Towel: You should carry a towel to wipe clean your golf balls and clubs.

Stretch fabric plasters: Plasters are not carried for any expected personal injuries, although sometimes sore fingers and heels may need attention. Temporary repairs to equipment can be made with this useful adhesive tape.

Book of rules: A book of rules is a must.

THE GOLF SHOT

The golf shot consists of four separate components:

Aim: This ensures that the ball will be sent in the desired direction.

Grip: This controls the club-head.

Stance: This ensures correct positioning and posture when making the shot.

Swing: This controls the plane of attack, and ensures that the ball is hit correctly.

All four components are important and each is dependent for effectiveness upon the other three. None can be neglected if the shot is to be effective. All deserve equal thought and practice, and are dealt with separately in the following pages.

THE AIM

'It's all in the mind' is a phrase used in many sports, particularly those like golf, where a stationary ball is to be hit. It leads to positive action. The idea is that you must imagine the shot to be played before addressing the ball, and you must be confident that you can make it. You picture the shot you are about to make – then make it.

Stand directly behind the ball looking towards the flag and imagine two clubs lying on the ground going away from you like railway tracks running from the ball towards the target. One line will be the target line for the ball, the other line will be for the correct positioning of the feet. Look for this target line. If you cannot see it, a simple exercise might help. Clench the fist of the right hand, and still standing behind the ball, gently swing the arm backwards and forwards as though you were going to throw a ball underhand along a line to the target. This action helps many beginners to see the imaginary line of flight.

Stand opposite the ball at right angles to the target. Place the club-head square behind the ball. You are now *addressing* the ball. The sole, or bottom of the club, will be sitting flat on the ground with the face square to the target, and you will be aiming correctly.

THE GRIP

The world's top golfers have one thing in common: a correct grip. Only through the correct grip can you control the club-head. The following descriptions assume a right-handed player, and obviously should be reversed for left-handers.

Many newcomers may find adopting the correct grip uncomfortable at first, but they should persevere. It will become a natural asset.

On forming the grip, it should be firm but not white-knuckle tight. The back of the left hand and the palm of the right hand point to the target and are square with it. Both hands must work together as one unit. The swing generates the power and passes it onto the club-head through the hands. Your club-head fires the ball to the target.

THE LEFT HAND

Place your feet together at right angles to the target, with the toes pointing towards the ball, so that the ball is on a line which would pass between your feet. Drop the left arm, keeping it firm, with the back of the left hand square to the hole.

With the club-head grounded behind the ball, place the club grip across the left hand. The butt (or the top of the club grip) will be lying snug along the palm. It is essential that the club is gripped by the fingers against the palms of the hands so that the wrist stays in a relaxed position, enabling a natural wrist-break to take place in the swing. You will see that the forefinger is underneath the grip as though about to pull a trigger. Now place the thumb on the top of the club grip and close the hand. The thumb and forefinger should be nearly level. The V created by the thumb and forefinger should be pointing between your head and right shoulder.

THE RIGHT HAND

With the right hand, the palm points towards the target. The two middle fingers must have the con-

When gripping the club, the back of the left hand and the palm of the right hand must point towards the target.

The grip should be laid across the middle two fingers, as these need to have control of the shot.

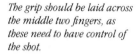

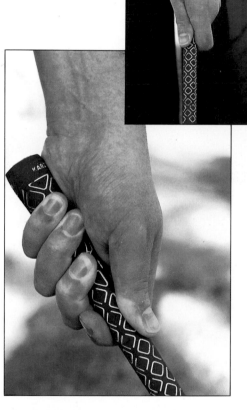

The club grip lies across the left hand. The heel of the hand is on the top of the grip and the forefinger underneath, as though you were pulling a trigger.

When the left hand is closed, the thumb and first finger should be level and the 'V' from the thumb and forefinger should point to the right shoulder.

When closing the right hand the left thumb is hidden. Both hands should grip the club with an even amount of pressure.

trol of the club. Let these two fingers grip the club and slide them up to meet the left hand, with the little finger overlapping the forefinger of the left hand. Now close the hand, with the thumb lying across the left hand side of the club grip. The V formed by the right thumb and the right forefinger should follow the same direction as the V on the left hand.

This grip is internationally known as the Vardon Grip, after its pioneer Harry Vardon, who between 1896 and 1914 won the British Open six times. Some beginners may discover that this grip is uncomfortable so an alternative must be tried. Two commonly used ones follow.

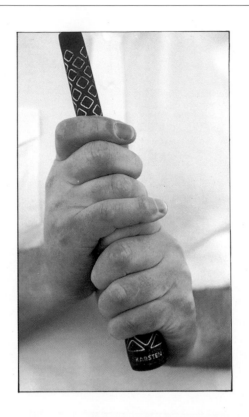

THE INTERLOCK GRIP

The left hand takes the same role as before, but when the right hand closes over the club grip the little finger of the right hand interlocks with the forefinger of the left hand. Instead of merely overlapping it, it comes between the first two fingers of the left hand, thus locking the hands together.

There is one other acceptable grip if you find you cannot feel comfortable with the first two.

THE DOUBLE-HANDED GRIP

Once again, the left hand takes the position on the club grip described before. To complete the grip, you bring in your right hand on to the club so that all four fingers of the right hand grip the club equally. The right thumb lies to the left of the club grip, completing a V pointing between the right-hand side of the head and the right shoulder. The palm of the right hand smothers the left thumb. This grip encourages excessive use of the hands, and unless the hands are kept as close together as possible, shots will start to go astray.

COMMON FAULTS

Two faults are common when gripping the club. The first is called a 'strong grip' and occurs when one of the hands (usually the right) slips round to the right hand side of the grip. This takes the palm off its square line to the target, and the V of the hand is now running up the right arm.

The club-face, in addressing the ball, may appear square to the target, but the hands are not. When the ball is struck, the tension created in the arms will bring the hands square to the target line but the club-face will be twisted. In effect, the club-face will have been closed, sending the ball left.

The other common fault is the 'weak grip', which occurs when one of the hands (usually the left) slips round the left hand side of the grip. The back of the left hand is now off the target line, although the club-head appears to be square. The V of the left hand will be running up the left arm. When the ball is struck, tension created in the arms will bring the hands square to the target line but, again, the club-face will be twisted. This time it will have been opened, and the result will be a wayward shot to the right.

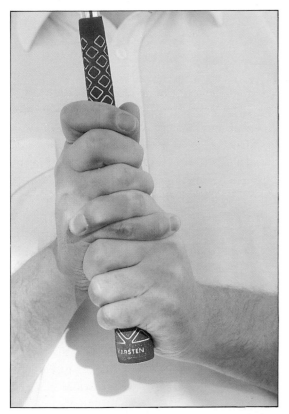

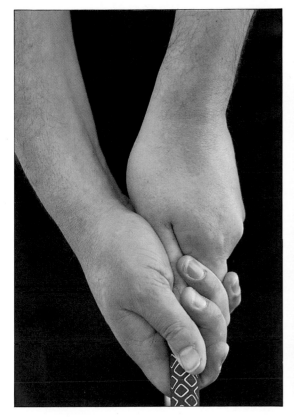

FAR LEFT: *The interlocking grip: the index finger of the left hand interlocks with the little finger of the right hand.*

LEFT AND INSET: *The double-handed grip: all eight fingers are on the club. When this grip is used, great care should be taken to keep the hands as close together as possible.*

FAR LEFT: *The strong grip: the 'V' of either hand (usually the right), points to the right shoulder. When the ball is struck, the hand becomes square, which closes the clubface.*

LEFT: *The weak grip: the 'V' formed by the thumb and forefinger points towards the left shoulder. When the ball is struck the hand becomes square and opens the clubface.*

RIGHT: When you take up the address position, the ball should be about an inch further forward for every club used, from the short-irons to the driver. The less loft on the club-face, the further forward the ball needs to be.

THE STANCE

The width between the feet at the stance is determined by the club chosen, which in turn depends on the type of shot to be played. The feet are closest together for the putting stroke, and they get farther apart as the shot gets longer, being at their widest for the drive.

Except for special awkward shots, the shoulders and hips should be square with the toes, which should be on a parallel line to the target line – or the 'railway track' as imagined when taking aim. The body weight will be evenly distributed between the feet.

The position of the stance in relation to the ball is also determined by the choice of club. There are two acceptable positions, the first favoured by beginners and the second by players with greater experience and confidence.

For beginners the address position varies through the range of shots from driver to wedge. Because the ball needs to be struck on the upward swing path, the drive should be addressed in line with the left heel.

The address position then moves forward about an inch (25 mm) for every club needed until, when you use the wedge, because you need to strike the ball at the bottom of the down swing, the address is made with the ball in line with the mid-point of the space between the feet.

The second address position is for the more confident golfer and is the one favoured by most golf professionals. All the shots are played with the ball lying opposite the inside of the left heel. With this method the feet are close together for the wedge shot, and the stance widens gradually for shots using clubs going up the range. So the driver would be taken with the ball still lying opposite the left heel, but the stance would have widened to shoulder width. When you are in the address position your hands should block your view of the shoelaces of the left shoe. If they do not, step back and take up your position again.

POSTURE

Your posture is your general bearing in the stance. Begin by imagining you are in the services and stand to attention. Stand straight, shoulders back and head up. Now bend over from the waist, keeping the back and legs straight. Push your bottom out and bend over one more notch. To release any tension, let your knees flex a little. Let your arms and hands hang down towards your left thigh, and grip the club. You are now in the address position.

THE ADDRESS POSITION

(1) Stand up straight with the shoulders back, the head up and arms at your sides.
(2) Keeping your back and legs straight, push your bottom out, bringing your head over towards the ball.
(3) Keeping your back straight, relax the tension in your knees.
(4) Now let your arms hang straight down, enabling you to swing your arms freely.
(5) Grip the club; you are now in the address position.

ABOVE: Nick Faldo assumes a square stance. Note the club lying on the ground to aid alignment during practice. Like most top professionals Nick Faldo finds aiming the shot the most consistently difficult thing to do properly. So when practising he gives himself a visual aid to the correct alignment. Apart from helping Faldo to aim the shot, the club on the ground shows him if his takeaway is starting in the proper direction and, if it is not, whether the club is going too far inside or outside the target line.

ABOVE: *To illustrate the role of the shoulders in the swing, hold a club across the upper chest (1). Turn the shoulders*

to the right (2) and back again to the left (3) without allowing the club to tilt toward the ground. This

demonstrates that when the shoulders turn, they rotate level with the ground.

THE BASIC SWING

Golf is played from a stationary position. Apart from croquet, there is no other game played outdoors with a club and a ball, in which the feet are kept in the same position throughout the stroke.

THE TURN

The fact that the feet do not move while the stroke is played has a tremendous limiting effect on the different directions in which you can move. If you are to keep your balance, the only way you can both move and create any real power is by turning. When you think of a turn, you think about turning around an axis. In the golf swing, the axis is not the spine, which is not attached to the ground, but the legs, the only parts of the body that are in contact with the ground. At the point of address, your weight is evenly distributed between both legs. On the turn of your backswing, your weight shifts on to your right leg, and on the turn of your downswing it moves to your left leg.

When you shift your weight and turn like this, you cannot keep your head still. The definition of a 'turn' as far as the golf swing is concerned is a twisting movement that keeps your shoulders level with the ground. If either shoulder drops at all, the movement you are making is a tilt and not a turn, and a tilt prevents a proper weight shift.

When you address the ball, both the ball and the club are in front of your body. Therefore, if you turn your body, the club will finish up behind it. When you make your backswing turn and turn your left shoulder over your right leg, the whole of your body weight will be transferred to your right leg. Then, when you make your downswing and swing the club back to the end of the follow-through, your body weight moves in the same direction as the club, supporting the hit and allowing your weight to flow freely on to your left leg into the follow-through. This is a very important sequence, as it allows the golfer to get all his weight into the stroke and to get the maximum energy into the ball.

When the body turns, the club also turns. So when the shoulders turn 90 degrees to the right in the backswing the face of the club will also have turned 90 degrees to the right. By the time the club has reached hip height and is parallel to the ground the toe of the club should be pointing vertically up into the air. Do not try to keep the club-face toward the target throughout the swing.

BACKSWING

The first movement of the backswing should be the pushing of the left hand and arm away from the target. It will feel as if the club is moving straight back, but, as the club is being swung in an arc around the shoulders, the club-head will come a little inside the target line almost immediately. If the backswing is checked when the club shaft is parallel to the ground, the shaft should also be parallel to the target line. This ensures that the plane of the swing is established on the target line. The plane is the angle between the ball and

LEFT: *By the time the club-head has reached shoulder height in the backswing (1), the shoulders will have been pulled around nearly 90 degrees, but the hips will have been left behind in the position they were at address (2). This movement stretches the muscles in the left side between shoulder and hip.*

the player's shoulders. No golfer has a choice of which plane to swing in, as this is determined by his height, the length of his arms and his distance from the ball. Once these criteria are established, the angle of the plane inevitably follows.

THE POWER SOURCE

The feeling of the first part of the backswing is of pushing the club straight back from the ball with the left hand and arm. By the time the club is horizontal to the ground at hip-height, the shoulders will have been pulled around by the swing of the left arm, but the hips will still be in their original address position and will not move until the turn of the shoulders pulls them around. This coiling of the muscles between the hips and the shoulders is a major power source, which is eliminated if the hips are turned too early. As the left arm continues to swing back, the shoulders are pulled around in front of the face. The left shoul-

straight line at address, they will remain so. There should be no change throughout the swing.

DOWNSWING

With the left hand and arm in line, the left hand lies above the right ready to dominate the downswing with a pull. Keeping the hands in this position ensures that the face of the club works within the plane of the swing that was established at address and all that is required of the downswing is that the club-face is fulled through the ball; no squaring up is necessary. You cannot pull the club squarely through the ball from a cupped-wrist position at the top of the backswing; you have to use the right hand to square up the club-face.

The backswing has concentrated effort on the top half of the body, and when you reach the top of the swing you will be mainly aware that the muscles on the left side between the shoulder and the hips are being stretched. In fact, how far you turn is less important than how far you stretch. A tall, slim person will use less hip turn than a shorter, stockier person. When the club is pushed back by the left hand and arm, the right elbow folds nicely into the side. Because the right elbow was pointing to the right hip at address, the right wrist is allowed to cock properly at the top of the backswing. The wider stance that was assumed at address helps to limit the amount of hip turn in the backswing, which means that at the top of the swing, the top half of the body is turning on a firmer platform.

THE SWING PLANE

The plane of the swing is the angle of the arc on which the club is swung. As we have seen the club is swung straight back from the ball, but, because the golfer stands to the side of the ball, the club is swinging around his body. The perfect illustration of this part of the golf swing was made by Anthony Ravielli in Ben Hogan's book *Modern Fundamentals of Golf.* Ravielli drew a pane of glass with a hole in it; the golfer's head came through the hole with the glass resting on his shoulders. The lower edge of the pane lay on the line along which the ball was going to be hit. When the club was swung,

LEFT: *The most graphic illustration of the plane of the swing. By imagining a pane of glass and the swinging of the club underneath it, the player is able to establish the correct angle at which to swing the club.*

ABOVE: *It is easy to see that it is necessary to swing the club at a shallow angle to prevent shattering the glass. The fact that the bottom of the pane of glass points to the target establishes the path the club-head should follow.*

tilt: this movement of the shoulders creates the weight shift on to the right side of the body. If you tilt your shoulders the weight drops vertically on to the left hip and leg and causes the reverse pivot.

At the end of the backswing the golfer should feel further from the ball because the left shoulder has not dropped. The hands should still be in the same position in relation to the arms as they were at address: if the left hand and arm were in a it swung underneath the pane of glass all the way through the backswing and all the way through the downswing as well. I believe that notwithstanding Hogan's many victories and the heights he reached to become such a magnificent striker, possibly his greatest contribution to golf was his analysis of the swing plane.

PULLING THROUGH THE BALL

The length of backswing is relatively unimportant. What is important is to turn the shoulders as far as possible while stretching the muscles on the left side. The shoulders usually turn about 90 degrees, and, if the muscles at the left side are fully stretched, the hips will turn between 30 and 45 degrees, nowhere near as much as the shoulders. When the hips are turned in this way, they pull the left leg across and toward the right leg, and the left heel comes slightly off the ground as the whole body weight is transferred to the right side. A supple person does not need to lift his left heel from the ground at all, but a stockier person may find that his heel needs to come up as much as 2 in (50 mm).

As the shoulders are pulled around at the start of the backswing, the club swings behind the body. The sooner the shoulders turn in the backswing, the sooner the club comes away from the target line and swings behind the player. If a player swings the club straight back from the ball directly along the target line, the line on which his arms are pulled in the backswing does not require him to turn his shoulders, and he will lift the club with just his arms and hands. This will lead to a very steep downswing, and the club will approach the ball from almost directly above it. Such a movement is a classic recipe for a slice or a topped shot. The shoulders should turn first in the backswing and drag the hips around only when the maximum stretch has been achieved by the muscles on the left side.

There is, in fact, no such thing as a 'position' at the top of the backswing. Instead the shoulders coil up and stretch the left side as far as they can, and then the downswing is started when the hips turn to the left and increase the stretch of the left side, eventually dragging the shoulders, then arms

and finally the club-head through the ball. The hips will return before the shoulders because they did not turn as far in the backswing. This initial pull moves the weight on to the left leg, and the hips continue to move the shoulders, arms and hands through the ball toward the target. The power source is now in the hips; so the club will try to find the plane around the hips that makes the club move downward and sets up a shallower attack on the ball.

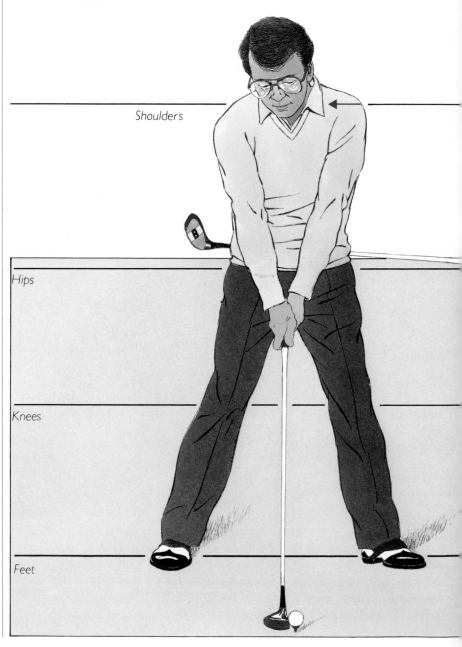

Shoulders

Hips

Knees

Feet

THE FULL SWING

During the downswing the dominant force is centrifugal. This means that the energy in the club travels along the shaft line. Force does not travel at right angles to the shaft; so it is not possible for the right hand to add power; it can only adjust the alignment of the face. Your head, meanwhile, must stay behind the ball until after impact; you will not be able to keep it totally still, of course,

but it must be behind the ball. Many of the very best players move their heads away from the target in the downswing because their bodies are setting up a force that opposes the pull of the arms.

POSITION OF FEET AND HIPS

As we have seen, the feet remain in the same place throughout the golf swing; therefore power is created by turning. The sensation during the downswing is of pulling the hips to the left, and

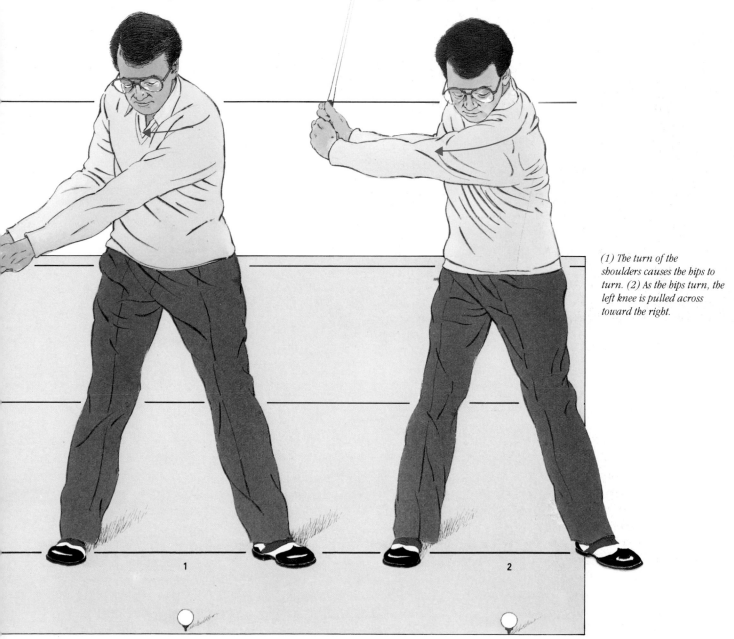

(1) The turn of the shoulders causes the hips to turn. (2) As the hips turn, the left knee is pulled across toward the right.

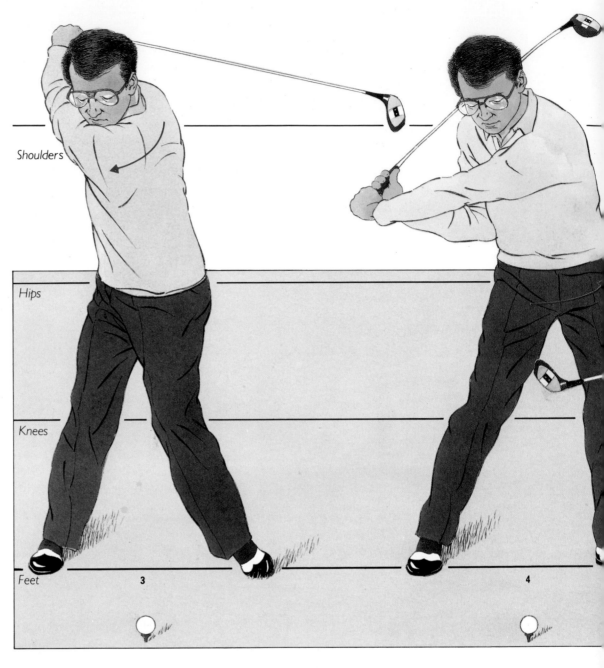

(3) The movement of the left knee will pull the left heel slightly off the ground.
(4) At the start of the downswing, the left knee straightens to accept the weight moving from the right leg. The unwinding of the hips pulls the right knee through the shot.

Shoulders

Hips

Knees

Feet

3

4

you should try to keep your hips as far ahead of the shoulders as they were at the top of the back-swing. At that point the ball is in front of you and the club-head behind you; so if all you do is pull with the left side the club must approach the ball from inside the target line.

THE IMPORTANCE OF A SHALLOW ATTACK

After impact, the hips keep pulling the club toward the target in a wide arc, and this delays the crossing over of the hands. The right hand will pass the left at about shoulder height on the follow-through as the arms swing around the shoulders, which

should be level at the end of the swing. The left side will be straight. The hands will be in the same relationship to the left shoulder at the end of the follow-through as they were to the right shoulder at the top of the backswing. During the through swing, attention focuses on the lower half of the body, the legs and the hips.

The shallow attack on the back of the ball is important because you are trying to hit the ball forward, and to hit the ball forward you must hit it on the back. A shallow attack allows you to do this. If you were to make a steep attack, the hit would be downward and power would be lost.

(5) The shoulders respond to the unwinding of the hips by maintaining a level plane as the club swings through the ball. The hips create the thrust of the downswing by turning to the left and transferring the weight to the left leg.
(6) The body weight is transferred from the right foot to the left during the downswing and, as the body clears, the right foot is pulled on to the toe.

In the course of the downswing the dominant force is centrifugal. This is the force that uncocks the wrists and widens the angle between the clubshaft and the left arm during the downswing. This uncocking action brings the club into a straight line, with the left arm directly below the left shoulder, and beyond that point the club-head swings past the hands.

When this happens and the arc begins to diminish, the club-head is pulled in against that force and slows down very quickly. The club-head accelerates only until the point that the left arm and the club shaft become a straight line; there,

the ball must be struck before this position is assumed. That is why, at address, it is an excellent idea to rehearse this position by gripping the club with the shaft tilted slightly forward and with the hands in front of the club-face and above the ball.

It is the first rule of golf that at the moment of impact the hands must be in front of the ball; they must be nearer to the target than the ball. Doing this guarantees that the club is accelerating into the ball at the moment of impact and therefore produces the most powerful blow that you can present to the ball. This can be achieved consistently only by pulling the club on to the ball.

THE RELEASE

Halfway through the downswing a player in the classic position will have fully cocked wrists and the toe of his club will be pointing up into the air. He is unwinding his body and turning it to the left so that the club will also turn to the left. Thus, at the corresponding position at shoulder height in the follow-through, the club will have turned through 180 degrees and the toe of the club will be pointing up in the air again. This is the action that many top players call 'the release', as it releases the club-face through the ball. This is a very important aspect of the golf swing, and, by learning to do it consistently, a player not only learns to hit the ball far and straight but also learns where the club-face is pointing through the critical area of the swing so that by making only slight adjustments he can slice to the right or hook to the left at will.

The head should stay behind the ball after the impact only until the turn of the shoulders pushes it up and the body straightens to become erect at the end of the follow-through. It is also necessary to lift the head at this point so that the flight of the ball can be watched.

When the shoulders turn away from the ball at the beginning of the backswing, a golfer may

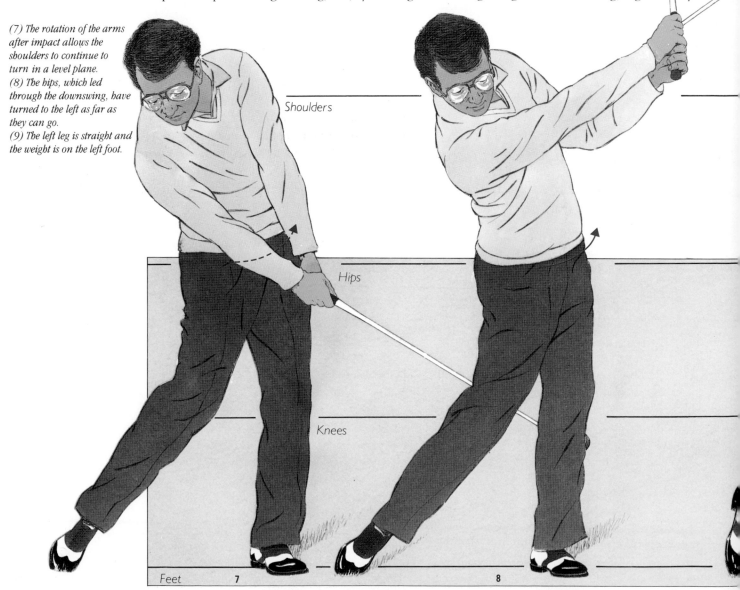

(7) The rotation of the arms after impact allows the shoulders to continue to turn in a level plane.
(8) The hips, which led through the downswing, have turned to the left as far as they can go.
(9) The left leg is straight and the weight is on the left foot.

Shoulders

Hips

Knees

Feet   7   8

feel that he is turning on an absolutely level plane. This is not so, however, because the spine is tilted forward at address and the shoulders turn at right angles to the spine. Nevertheless the idea of turning in a level plane helps to keep the left shoulder up and keeping the left shoulder high and turning it causes the club-face to open naturally in the backswing, and allows the player to keep the club within the plane of the swing. The left shoulder stays up as it turns into the backswing, and it follows

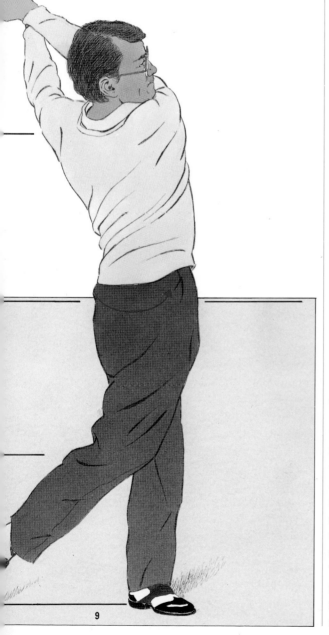

that during the downswing the right shoulder will not be pulled down but will instead be pulled around the head in the same plane that the left shoulder took in the backswing. This position will make the player more aware of his arms swinging down and through the ball into the follow-through.

When the body weight is established on the left side and the hips have turned to the left in the downswing, the right leg is also pulled through the shot. This action causes the right heel to lift off the ground just before impact, and no attempt should be made to keep it clamped on the ground. At the end of the classic swing, the right foot should not be carrying any weight, and the heel should be vertically above the toes.

The power in the swing is created by stretching the muscles down the left side. The more the hips are left behind in the address position while the shoulders make their maximum 90 degree turn, the tighter the muscles are drawn and the more recoil there will be in the downswing. The purpose of the downswing is to turn the left hip and maintain the stretch in the left side so that that at impact the left side is stretched just as much as it was at the top of the backswing.

ROLE OF THE HANDS AND WRISTS

The role of the hands, or rather, the action of the wrists, throughout the golf swing is of great importance. The takeaway is performed with the left hand pushing the club away from the target. As the shoulders turn and the right elbow folds into the right side, the wrists cock to accommodate this movement. At the top of the backswing the angle between the left arm and the club shaft is usually about 90 degrees, because the back of the left arm and the back of the left hand are in the same relationship to each other as they were at address. When the left hip starts the downswing towing of the left shoulder and arm, the weight of the club-head forces the wrists to cock even more. This extra cock at the start of the downswing helps to create a late hit. It eliminates the early throw of the club with the right hand, which is the bane of many a handicapped golfer. The greater the wrist cock at this point in the downswing, the later the release will be into the ball, and the further the ball can be hit. This is the explanation for why many slightly built or short players can out-hit even the tallest golfers: they are unable to uncock their wrists late in the downswing.

This uncocking is not a conscious movement. The pull of the left arm and the centrifugal force working upon it automatically uncock the wrists. The extra cocking at the start of the downswing merely delays the moment before centrifugal force gets to work. The later the hit through the ball, the later in the follow-through the clubhead passes the hands, and the later the crossover point. This is another factor in great shot-making accuracy. There is no doubt that the greatest players are those who hit the ball with the latest possible release of the wrists through the impact area.

After the hands have crossed over, they swing naturally around the player's shoulder as far as they can go to the end of the swing. At no point of the downswing is there a conscious hit with the right hand.

LONG SWINGS AND SHORT SWINGS

The length of the backswing is not of great consequence. Far more important is how much you stretch the left side of your body. Swinging the club back until the shaft is horizontal to the ground at the top of the backswing does not make any difference at all. In general, the longer the swing, the higher the ball is hit, and the shorter the swing, the more the ball seems to be propelled forward, which is the way it needs to be propelled if maximum distance is to be attained.

To get the club back into a horizontal position, most golfers either have to let go of the grip, over-turn their hips or lift their left foot off the ground so that it rests only on the very tip of the toes at the top of the backswing. These are all faults. A player with a shorter swing has the club under control at all times and is able to concentrate on swinging the club forward and into a long follow-through rather than having to recover from a faulty backswing position.

Among the longer swingers over the last 15 to 20 years are renowned professionals such as Tom Watson, Johnny Miller and Ben Crenshaw. Nevertheless, while all three of them are brilliant iron players, none could be described as a consistent driver. This is because the long swing that they feel they need to give them distance also makes them erratic. When they use shorter shafts in their irons, the swing becomes controllable and they are brilliant. I do not suppose anybody has hit good iron shots more consistently than Johnny Miller did in the early 1970s. He did not just hit the ball close to the hole, he used to lean it against the flagstick.

However, if you compare the number of fairways hit by Miller, Watson and Crenshaw, with those hit by Peter Jacobsen, Doug Sanders and Lee Trevino, probably three of the game's shortest swingers, Jacobsen, Sanders and Trevino will have hit twice as many fairways as the other three players. In fact, they are still able to play more attacking shots to the green because they play from the short grass of the fairways almost all of the time. If the longer swingers all hit the ball 100 per cent and the shorter swingers all hit the ball 10 per cent, the longer swingers would probably hit the ball further over the course of a round, but the shorter swingers would drive more shots onto the fairway.

THE MODERN SWING

Swing the club away from the ball with your left hand and arm and turn your shoulders as far as you can before allowing your hips to move. When you feel you are losing balance or you have to let go of the club to keep it going further, that is the point at which your backswing should stop. As long as your arms get up to about shoulder height and your shoulders turn as far as they can while stretching your left side away from your hip, that is as long a backswing as you need, because you are still in control of the club. Pull with your left side and keep your left hand in front of the clubhead throughout impact, and you will hit the ball as the club accelerates, and that means that you will be transmitting the maximum power and achieving the maximum distance.

There are only two ways to move an object – you can push it or you can pull it. In golf it is essential that you pull your club through the ball if you want to achieve consistency and power. This is the modern swing, evolved by trial and error over the years by the game's greatest players. It is a method that does not let them down in the pressures of tournament play. It is the method that allows them consistently, day in and day out, to compete for the huge amounts of money that are available to the top players these days.

THE WEIGHT SHIFT

It is worth spending more time on the shifting of weight during the swing. As the club is swung back from the ball by the left arm and shoulder at the beginning of the backswing, the movement of the club to the right should take the body weight firmly across on to the right side. By the time the club has been swung to hip height, 80 per cent of the body weight is firmly on the right foot.

This move must be established right at the start of the backswing to ensure that the right leg is a firm foundation on which the upper body can turn. As long as the left shoulder turns on a plane level with the ground, the single movement of turning the left shoulder across and over the right leg will transfer the weight to the right leg. As we want the shoulder to turn to be complete by the time the hands have swung up to shoulder height, this movement must be completed in the first half of the backswing. At the top of the backswing the weight must be on the right side so that, when the arms are swung forward through the ball on the downswing, the body weight is moving in the same direction as the club, thereby supporting the hit and making the strength of the strike much more solid. This weight shift also helps to keep the body erect throughout the stroke.

Many golfers resist this weight movement to the right side because when they do make the correct movement, they feel as if they are swaying to the right. Remember, in a golf swing, because your feet are anchored, the only way you can move to make any energy at all in the backswing is with a turn, and if you are turning with your weight on your right leg you cannot possibly sway.

BELOW: *(1) As the club is swung away from the ball, the club-face will rotate with the turn of the shoulders. (2) Halfway back, the shoulders and the club-face will both have turned 90 degrees.*

This rotation of the blade helps to keep the left shoulder high and in the downswing, will allow the player to release the right side through the shot.

(3) The turn of the shoulders brings the club inside the target line. This turning action keeps the right arm close to the side of the body, which is a very strong position.

If the left shoulder does not stay high as it turns into the backswing but tilts down toward the ground, the right hip will be forced to move to the right, thereby taking away the height that your body has established at address and moving the centre of your arc closer to the ground. This will cause you to hit the ground behind the ball. Because the left shoulder has dropped and the right hip slid to the right at the top of the backswing, the weight has been dropped down through the left hip on to the left foot, and the body will be bowed out to the right with the weight on the left foot – there will have been no weight shift to the right.

The weight shift to the right causes the downswing to become shallow and enables you to attack the ball with the club travelling in a much wider arc. Again, the weight shift to the right will give a feeling of having more room to swing in, and enables your arms to swing more freely.

When the weight shift is properly executed, it requires that the lower half of the body, the legs and the hips are used properly. Players often say that they cannot use their legs in the golf swing, and they never will until they learn to shift their weight properly. As soon as they learn to transfer their weight to the right leg in the backswing and through onto the left leg in the follow-through, their leg action will fall into place.

WEIGHT SHIFT'S EFFECT ON TEMPO

A good weight shift also gives the golf swing a constant tempo. It is very easy to swing the club too quickly if you are swinging only with your arms and hands, but it is very difficult to shift the mass of your weight quickly as this has to be done by the large muscles in the body. The weight shift acts as a governor on the pace at which you can swing to the top of the backswing because it takes

(4) Halfway through the downswing in the perfect position the wrists are fully cocked and the toe of the club points straight up in the air.
(5) To use this position properly, the golfer has to rotate the arms as the wrists uncock.
(6) By the time the club has reached shoulder height in the follow-through, it will have turned to the point where the toe is pointing up in the air again.

This rotation of the club-face is known as the release. The full release of the clubface in this manner gives power and direction to the shot. It also ensures that after impact, the club stays in the plane used for the back- and downswings.

so long for the weight to shift on to the right leg and because the weight shift has to be complete by the time the hands are at shoulder height in the backswing. The time taken to make a hand swing up to shoulder height is kept at a constant, slow pace to allow the body time to make the weight shift. When the weight shift is complete, the shoulders and arms coil tighter up to the top of the backswing.

The downswing is initiated when the left hip pulls to the left and the weight is pulled on to the left leg. This is also an action that takes place relatively slowly, and it allows the club-head, which is still moving back, to tighten the coil even more as the lower body starts down. When the weight is established and balanced on the left leg, it acts as a solid base from which the club can be pulled

(7) At the finish of the swing the club lies over the left shoulder at the same angle it lay over the right shoulder at the top of the backswing.

through the ball in the downswing. This is one reason why the hips must turn in the downswing and not move laterally to the left, for if they do, they tend not to take the weight with them. Instead, the weight remains on the right leg, which causes the right shoulder to drop behind the ball. When this happens, the hit becomes a scoop. The follow-through is created by the hands and arms becoming disconnected from the body and being lifted over the head. This exaggeratedly high position forces the body into the incorrect reverse-C position. Ensuring that the downswing is made predominantly by the hips turning to the left, the body will stay upright. As the body remains upright the weight is transferred more freely on to the firm left leg.

The importance of the weight shift is being increasingly understood and is being taught by the more discerning of the top teaching professionals. It is an entirely natural movement. If you were to throw a stone, you would shift your weight without thinking about it.

ABOVE: *Seve Ballesteros is capable of hitting more different kinds of shots to order than any other golfer in the world. His swing control is so good that he is able to alter the alignment of the club-face slightly and produce any type of flight a shot requires.*

PLAYING WOODS AND IRONS

THE DRIVER

We have looked at the full swing. Now we will look at the shots that can be produced with it. The first shot in golf is the drive, and that is where we will begin.

The first thing to say about the drive is that it is probably the easiest shot in golf in that you are standing on level ground, you can decide from which part of the tee you want to play, the ball is sitting up waiting to be hit, and the fairway is the largest target you have on the golf course. Driving is difficult, however, because most of the time you are trying to hit the ball as far as you can. This means that you are exposing your swing to maximum pressure. In addition, the driver has the straightest face of all the golf clubs and, because you hit the ball on its 'equator', the straight face allows you to impose side-spin on the ball far more easily than you could impose back-spin. (To produce back-spin you have to hit the ball at the 'bottom'.) Therefore, although the conditions in which you start are the best you can give yourself, the demands of the shot probably put the player under as much pressure as anything else on the golf course. It is tempting to let your physical strength overpower your golfing technique because you are trying to hit the ball as far as you can. This is folly: to produce distance you must swing the club as fast as you can, and you cannot move the club any faster than you can swing it.

TEE HEIGHT

The first practical question is, how high do you tee the ball? The minimum height at which the ball must be teed is that at which half of it is visible above the crown of the driver. The crown is the top of the driver's head. This allows you to sweep the ball up into the air and increase the effective loft on the club when you are hitting. You

The correct way to tee the ball is to push the tee in the ground so that half the ball is visible above the top of the driver.

are trying to drive the ball a long way; so you want to eliminate as much back-spin as possible. By teeing the ball up into the air, you are able to hit up behind it and hit slightly over the ball to minimize the back-spin. Moreover, by teeing the ball high, you are able to move it further to the left in your stance, thereby allowing yourself more down-swing to use to strike the ball. Modern drivers have 12 degrees angle of loft on the club-face. In the old days, drivers were made with 8 or 9 degrees of loft on the face, and it was therefore important to tee the ball up high so that you could add to the effective loft by driving the ball up into the air. You are going for maximum distance, and the desire to overpower the shot is great: you have to discipline yourself to create the same technique of using your weight to add power to the stroke of the driver that you learned in the previous chapter.

(1) Because the ball is teed above the ground, at address it should be positioned more toward the left foot. This is so the ball can be struck at a point in the arc where the club is starting to swing up. Striking the ball on the upswing gives the shot less back-spin and therefore more forward momentum.

(2) The effect of having the ball teed up and further forward in the stance allows the player to sweep the club back more around the body, forcing the right elbow closer to the side.

(3) Swinging the club around the body in this manner increases the shoulder turn and coils the left side to the maximum.

Driving is golf's offensive shot. It is a shot that, provided it is played properly, completes approximately half the hole in perfect position. A first-rate shot with a driver on a par 4 leaves the shortest possible club to play for the second shot and, on a par 5, often brings the green within range of the second shot.

Many golfers are frightened to hit with a number 1 wood, and they prefer to take their chances with a 2, or even these days a 3, wood from the tee. This is taking away one of the great joys of the game. To see a properly driven ball hanging up in the air, travelling forward as far as you know you can hit it out of the middle of the club, is one of the great thrills of golf.

The idea of hitting a 3 wood and leaving the ball in play is all very well for the top tournament professional, who is quite capable of hitting a driver but has picked the part of the fairway he wants the ball to land. For the average golfer, that

Viewed from behind it is clear that the club has been swung around the body and the weight has been transferred on to the right leg (4). The body is fully turned behind the ball . As the club approaches the ball in the downswing the pull of the hips is apparent.
The toe of the club points up in the air before being squared up at impact by the uncocking of the wrists. The right elbow is close to the body, indicating that the hit will be made from inside the target line (5). At impact the hips have continued to turn to the left and the uncocking of the wrists has squared up the club-face.

The correct finish to the swing has the player in a relaxed position, his left side straight and his hips and shoulders horizontal to the ground (6).

Viewed from the front it is evident that the body has stayed behind the ball, thereby allowing the player to strike the ball squarely in the back (4, 5). The body should not be allowed to straighten until after impact, and at the finish of the swing the body is erect and facing the target (6). This finish can be achieved only by the correct rotation of the hands and arms through the ball.

is just laziness, because he has not bothered to develop the skill to play the game properly.

When you watch great drivers such as Jack Nichlaus, Greg Norman or Ian Woosnam, and you see the prodigious distances that they drive the ball, you can understand how they bring in scores in the low and middle 60s. This is one skill in golf that distinguishes the great tournament professionals from the top-class amateurs. Very few amateurs develop their golfing muscles to the point that they can generate the speed that these great players can. Norman, particularly, is one of the longest straight hitters of all time.

Apart from the wedges and the putter, the driver is the most frequently used club in the bag. Therefore, it makes good sense to find a driver that you like, and that you feel you can use and make a friend of.

It is far easier to follow through with the driver than it is with any of the other clubs in the bag because the ball is teed up. You are striking the ball with the club already swinging up toward the follow-through, and you are using maximum power. Therefore, the momentum of the club will make the follow-through longer, and at the end of the swing the shaft of the driver will be lying across your shoulders behind you.

FAIRWAY WOODS

The fairway woods are numbers 3, 4 and 5, and the difference in distance between is only about 12 yards (11 m) a club. The technique for using the fairway woods differs from the technique for the driver in that the ball is sitting on the ground and you have to sweep the ball forward and off the turf to make it fly. A shot with the 3 wood is therefore the most dangerous shot in golf because it has the least amount of loft on it necessary to make the ball fly up into the air. The lie in which you find the ball before you play your 3 wood is critical. If the ground is very bare and the lie very tight, or if the opposite occurs, and the ball lies cupped in the grass, it is better not to play the 3 wood at all, but to consider the 4 or 5 woods, which have more loft and will elevate the ball more quickly.

The 4 wood is a good club to use from the fairway or from a good lie in the semi-rough; the 5 wood is a good club to use from semi-rough or for any shots that require a high trajectory, perhaps over bunkers or over water, into the green from around the 200 yards (180 m) mark. With both the 4 and 5 woods the sweeping action of the club through the ball elevates it into the air. You must not try to lift the ball into the air with these clubs; you will end up topping the ball if you do. If anything, the ball should be struck with a slightly downward blow, in the same way that you would strike down slightly on the long irons.

Many tournament players use the 3 wood from the tee to obtain extra control. Sometimes, when they are laying up on a very narrow hole, the extra back-spin that is generated by the more lofted 3 wood will keep the ball straighter than the same shot with a driver and they are prepared to sacrifice 15–20 yards (14–18 m) distance from the driver shot for the extra control they get with a 3 wood.

When playing the 3 wood from the tee, the ball should be teed just on top of the grass to duplicate the sort of situation that would obtain if the ball were in the perfect lie on the fairway. This way, the approach to the shot can be the same as it would be out of the fairway – that is, it should be possible to sweep the ball forward off the top of the turf rather than either swinging up at it if the ball were teed up too high or having to chop down on it if the ball were down in the grass.

The 4 and 5 woods can be played from the tee on long par 4 holes, and it is possible to re-create a good lie on the turf with them as well. Therefore, you should tee the ball just on top of the grass and sweep the ball forward off it when you swing.

The 6 and 7 woods have become popular over the last few years, particularly with women golfers and men who are not strong enough to

The shorter shaft of the fairway wood creates a slightly more upright swing plane, which makes it easier for the player to hit the ball into the air (2). The wide sole on the bottom of the fairway wood allows the ball to be played further back in stance without the fear of the club-head digging into the ground (3).

The fairway wood shot is the
longest shot to be played off the
ground. The ball should be
positioned more toward the
centre of the stance (1) than
with the driver as the club
should be at the bottom of its arc
when it makes contact with the
ball. Because the fairway wood
is slightly shorter than the driver,
the player will stand closer to the
ball (2).

The rear view of the fairway wood shot is exactly the same as that of the driver (4), except that the ball is positioned further back in the stance and struck at the bottom of the arc (5). Fairway woods should be used only when the ball is sitting up reasonably well on the grass.

handle the long irons. These clubs are played in exactly the same way as the 4 and 5 woods. They are popular because they will guarantee the trajectory that a long iron will not if you want to play a high dropping, stopping shot from 170–190 yards (155–170 m). You will be able to sweep the ball away more successfully with a wood than punch it with an iron, which gives a high, arching shot while the iron is driven forward lower.

However, whichever club is used, there should be no change in swing technique. The club should be swung away from the ball with the

left arm and hand, while the left shoulder is pulled around, stretching the muscles in the left side until they are so tight that the left hip is forced to turn a little too. The weight is transferred on to the right leg in the backswing, and the downswing is started by turning the left hip to the left and maintaining, or even tightening, the stretched left side and pulling the club through with the left arm to the end of the follow-through.

When you are using the fairway woods, the ball should be positioned half-way between the left heel and the centre of the stance.

LEFT: *Because the club meets the ball at the bottom of the swing arc, the extra loft will impart more back-spin and guarantee a higher trajectory to the shot (6). The average golfer usually finds long irons difficult to play and prefers to use a fairway wood. For the reason, 6 and 7 woods have enjoyed increased popularity. The technique for playing these is exactly the same as for the longer fairway woods.*

BELOW: *The temptation to scoop the ball into the air must be resisted (5). The lie of the ball must be carefully assessed before the player selects the correct fairway wood. The tighter the ball is lying to the ground, the more lofted the club should be.*

IRON SHOTS

In a normal set of 14 clubs, which is all that you are allowed under the Rules of Golf, golfers tend to carry three wooden clubs and a putter. This means that the maximum number of irons that can be used is 10, which are normally the 2, 3, 4, 5, 6, 7, 8, 9 and the pitching wedge and sand wedge. Some people, however, prefer to add a third wedge, usually a more lofted wedge, of 60 degrees, in place of a 2 iron, which for many amateurs is extremely difficult to hit well constantly. A lot of amateurs opt for a fourth wood instead of either an extra wedge or a 2 iron.

The ball is played just forward of the centre of the stance because it is vital that the hands are ahead of the blade, both at address and at impact. Increasing the amount that you push your hands forward increases the amount of back-spin that can be imparted to the golf ball. Irons are the clubs that give the greatest accuracy; therefore, the more back-spin you can impart to the ball when you strike it with an iron, the straighter the ball is going to fly, and the back-spin helps when the ball lands.

LENGTH OF SHAFT

As the numbers on the irons get higher, the shaft gets shorter; this means that with the higher number irons, you have to stand a little closer to the ball. Again this helps you to hit down on the ball and create the back-spin that is so necessary on these shots. You have to stand closer to the ball and, without having to do anything else, your swing automatically becomes more upright. This is a result of the shorter shaft, not of any conscious alteration in your swing technique. Because you are looking for accuracy, you do not have to hit the ball as hard as you possibly can, only sufficiently hard to make it travel the distance you require. One of the keys to consistent iron play is to keep the tempo smooth; if you hit a 6 iron 160 yards (145 m), you should hit every 6 iron 160 yards. If you have to hit the ball 170 yards (155 m) you need to use a 5 iron, not to take a harder swing with the 6.

The shafts of the irons are shorter than those

of the woods, and you may find that when you keep your hands leading as you go through the ball, you shave the grass with the club as it keeps descending to the bottom of its arc after you have hit the ball. This is a good sign, and is an excellent way of checking whether your club is swinging toward the target or not. After you have hit the ball, stand behind the divot and look to see which way it points. It should point either toward the target or very slightly to the left of it. A divot that points to the right of the target is no good to anyone and means that the shot has been pushed.

A full set of irons comprises nine clubs. They are the 3, 4, 5, 6, 7, 8 and 9, the pitching wedge and sand iron. The 3 iron has the least amount of loft on the face and the sand iron the most. The 3 iron is the longest club and the pitching wedge and the sand iron the shortest. The differences between each club is about four degrees in loft and ½ inch (12 mm) in length. Additions to the standard set are the 1 and 2 irons and a 60 degree wedge. The distances achieved with each club will depend on the player's ability, but the difference between each club should be constant.

SHORT IRONS

When you are playing the high-numbered irons, numbers 7, 8 and 9 or the wedges, you are looking for so much accuracy that you do not really want to make a full swing. A three-quarter swing, keeping your rhythm, will give you the accuracy that you require. Remember, when you use iron shots, you are looking for accuracy, not power. In addition, because the shafts are shorter with these clubs, the divot will be the deepest. No divot should ever be much more than a ¼ in (6 mm) into the ground but it will always be most notice-able after you have struck the ball with these clubs. When you are playing iron shots, pull the club through the ball toward the target. Always keep the target in mind and always make sure that your swing goes toward it. Then, even a ball that is not hit exactly in the middle of the club will fly in that direction.

LONG IRONS

Long irons are the most difficult clubs to use because they require the same sort of technique that is used with the fairway woods. You must

ABOVE: *The technique required to play a 2 iron is the same as for a fairway wood. The ball should be positioned just to the left of the centre of the stance to ensure that it is struck at the bottom of the swing arc. The shaft in the 2 iron is shorter than that of the 3 wood,* which allows the player to swing in a slightly more upright plane.

INSET: *The loft of the club produces a climbing, soaring shot, which stops more quickly than a fairway wood shot.*

ABOVE: *The 6 iron is 2 inches (50 mm) shorter than the 2 iron and is designed for accuracy. This club should never be used for maximum distance as control is paramount. The ball position is, again, at the bottom of the swing arc.*

INSET: *Because the club shows plenty of loft to the player, the temptation is not to scoop the ball into the air but to chop down on it. This action negates the loft and produces an incorrect lower trajectory.*

ABOVE: *The wedge is designed totally for accuracy and distance should never be a factor. It should never be used from more than 100 yards (90 m) from the target. The technique required is usually less than a full swing, which means the shoulders turn but the movement of the lower body is restricted.*

INSET: *The loft on the wedge enables the ball to be hit at a much higher trajectory.*

make a good hard swing at the ball and have a long follow-through, pulling the club toward the target along the way. Long irons are difficult to play because they lack the loft of the other irons; therefore, the amount of back-spin imparted to the ball is less and the ball does not rise into the air as easily as it would with, say, a 4 or 5 iron. In addition, because less back-spin is imparted to the ball, the chances of getting side-spin increse, and it is not as easy to hit the ball straight with a long iron as it is with a middle iron.

However, if you practice hard and keep on pulling the club through toward the target whenever you play, you'll soon become a proficient long-iron player.

These days many top tournament golfers prefer to hit a 1 iron from the tee than play a driver on very tight holes or holes that do not need the full distance from the tee. They hit a 1 iron because the shorter shaft gives them greater control over the ball, and a 1 iron has 6 or 7 degrees more loft than a driver. It is consequently easier to control a straight shot because of the extra back-spin that is imparted, and top players can usually hit the ball with a 1 iron within 15–20 yards (14–18 m) of their longest drive. Although the 1 iron and the 3 wood have a similar amount of loft, the iron, with its shorter shaft, tends to be driven forward or lower trajectory with more back-spin, while the 3 wood tends to be swept into the air, where it is more vulnerable to the wind and the elements.

The irons are the scoring clubs in golf. Any player who hits irons well will find more greens with his second shots.

THE 2 IRON SWING

A perfectly played 2 iron can provide one of the greatest pleasures in golf. Because of its lack of loft a 2 iron shot should only be attempted from the fairway but with a sound swing technique this club can soon be mastered.

RIGHT: *(1) The technique for the 2 iron is a balanced address position with the hands slightly ahead of the ball.*

(2) The takeaway is initiated by the left arm and shoulder turning over the right leg.

(3) At the top of the backswing the weight is coiled on the right side of the body. The hips have turned only a minimum amount and the left heel is slightly off the ground.

(4) The unwinding of the hips is started by transferring the weight on to the left leg.

(6) The head is behind the ball to enable the golfer to swing away from himself and toward the target. At shoulder height in the follow-through the hips have turned as far as they can, and the hands have released the club-face in plane through the ball.

(5) Approaching impact, the hips are continuing to unwind and the weight is now almost totally transferred on to the left leg.

(7) At the end of the swing the weight is totally on the left leg and the right foot, which bears no weight, is balanced on the toe.

Greg Norman, a consummate long-iron player, at the top of his swing. This most powerful player has made a huge shoulder turn in order to create the power he needs to execute this shot. Because of his great length Greg Norman can attack any course he plays, which suits his confident Australian nature. Although his game is based on power, Norman is a fine short game player and a particularly good putter. He is a superb player, who has worked hard at his game and continues to do so.

THE 6 IRON SWING

The 6 iron is the classic middle-iron club. Most golfers are confident with a 6 iron because it is usually the club they learn to play with when they start. It has a fair amount of loft but not too much and gives a satisfactory flight to the ball.

(1) At address the shorter shaft on the 6 iron requires that the player bends over a little more from the waist.

(2) This means that the club is taken back straighter along the target line and less around the body.

(3) This is a result of the shorter shaft and should not be a conscious move on the part of the player.

(4) As this is an accuracy club, rhythm and tempo are of prime importance, and the weight shift on the backswing will act as governor on the pace of the swing.

(5) *The start of the downswing should not be hurried. The weight should be transferred smoothly on to the left leg, and this will set up a chain reaction which will pull the club through the ball in a rhythmic manner.*

(6) *The follow-through will not be as long because the club has not been swung so fast.*

(7) *Therefore, it should be easier to maintain balance at the finish. The essence of a 6-iron shot is to hit the ball a particular distance and direction without undue effort.*

7

Ian Woosnam at the top of the swing with a 6 iron. He has reaped the benefits of hard work on the practice tee perfecting possibly the most simple method used by any of today's top stars. Although only 5 feet 5 inches (1.64 m) tall, Woosnam's swing is quite upright because he swings the club straight back from the ball. This allows his shoulders to turn fully while restricting his hip turn to a minimum. He has very strong hands and arms and is able to hit the ball very hard without seeming to apply much effort. This easy rhythm is what makes Woosnam's swing look so simple.

USING A WEDGE

After the putter, the wedge is used more than any other club in the bag: practice with this club is therefore important. The shorter shaft and extra loft are designed to promote accuracy, and power is not required.

(1) When the wedge is used, the stance to the ball is closer because of the shorter shaft, and this creates a more upright swing plane. The weight is equally balanced on both feet.

(2) The swing commences when the weight is shifted onto the right leg. The club is swung back by the turn of the shoulders, and there is no independent hand action. The right arm is folded close into the right side.

(3) Because accuracy is required and the swing plane is more upright, there is less body turn and more arm swing. The wrists are kept firm, and the backswing is a little shorter than it would be if full power were required. The body is perfectly balanced behind the ball, with the weight on the right leg while the left heel remains in contact with the ground.

(4) The downswing is initiated by the left hip turning to the left and thereby transferring the weight to the left foot. This stretches the muscle between the left hip and left shoulder and means that the hips are ahead of the shoulders. The wrists are still fully cocked, which keeps the right arm close to the right side. The head is behind the ball, and the initial unwinding of the hips has started to draw the right heel from the ground.

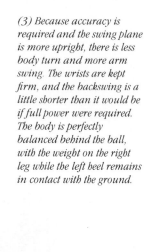

(5) At impact the body is balanced on the left foot, and the hands, which are pulling the club, are ahead of the ball. The left hip is still turning to the left, and the right leg is thrusting toward the target, which allows the club to be swung and held on the target line longer. This is the great advantage of having a wide stance. The hands leading in this manner ensure that the ball is struck before the turf.

(6) After the ball has been struck, the club continues to move toward the target. When the wedge is used, the hands do not cross over as early in the follow-through, which creates a wider arc through the ball. This is essential for accuracy. The weight is now totally on the left leg, and the head is just starting to come up as the body is straightening.

(7) At the finish of the swing the left side is straight and the hips and shoulders are level with the ground. The right foot rests vertically on the toe and, because no power has been put into the swing, the club has not swung past the head in the follow-through.

Tom Wieskopf demonstrates the classic top-of-the-swing position with a wedge. He has achieved this position by turning his shoulders and restricting his hip movement. Weiskopf had the most natural, elegant, powerful swing of any of the top professionals competing over the last 25 years. British Open Champion in 1973, his successes were limited because of his fiery temperament. There was no more awe-inspiring sight in golf than Wieskopf playing well but a poor bounce, a slight mishit would ruin the hole, the round and, sometimes, the day. His swing was long, free and powerful.

High-speed photography reveals the moment of truth when an iron strikes a golf ball. The amount the ball is compressed is dictated by the speed at which the club strikes it, but the primary effect of an iron shot is the back-spin put on the ball. Back-spin provides control over the shot and creates a straighter flight. When the ball is compressed between the grooves on the club and the grass, back-spin is created to provide aerodynamic efficiency. Golf balls are made in three types of compression – 80, 90 and 100. Compression will vary according to the type of ball used: the softer the ball (80) the easier it is to compress. The cover and construction of the ball also affects back-spin velocity. Two-piece Surlyn-covered balls leave the club-face at approximately 7,000 revolutions per minute while a wound, Balata-covered ball will leave the club-face at 9,000 rpm.

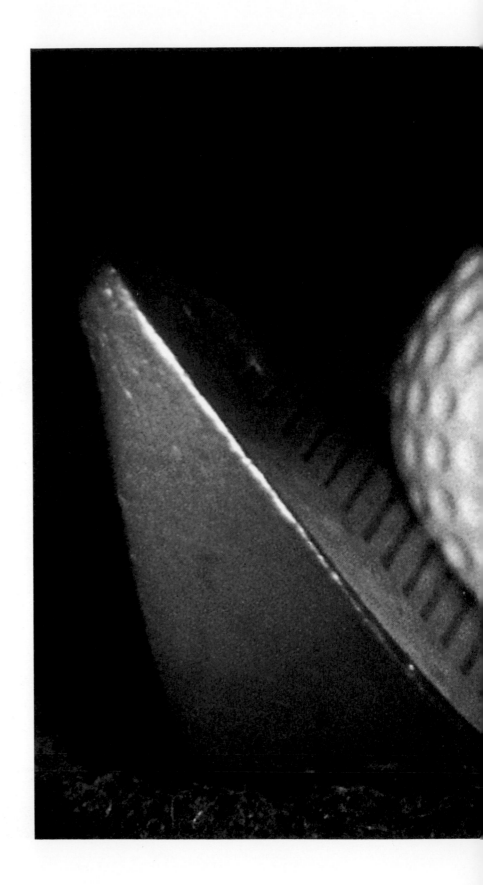

THE SHORT GAME

So far we have assumed that, either from the tee or the fairway, you have approached the green with a long-range shot and succeeded. However, there are bound to be occasions when your approach shot lands up just short or wide of the green, whether by accident or design, and you are not close enough or the ground is not good enough for you to use your putter. (This club should always be the first choice, wherever possible.)

When faced with this situation, your objective should be to get the ball as close to the hole as you can, thus hopefully saving you that extra putt and another stroke at the hole. To do this, you need to play either a pitch shot or a chip shot.

The basic difference between these shots is that when pitching you list the ball well up in the air and aim to make it stop quickly on landing. When chipping, there is less height on the ball and more run. In principle you should play the former the further away you are from the hole and the latter the closer you are to the hole.

THE CHIP SHOT

When you are chipping you want the ball to roll as much as possible because the rolling ball has more chance of going into the hole. You need to conceive a shot that flies as low as possible before it hits the ground. Therefore, most chip shots are played within 5 yards (4.5 m) of the edge of the green. As you want minimum flight and maximum roll, this shot should be played with a 5, 6 or 7 iron and the technique is described below.

Stand close to the ball and try to get your eyes as nearly over the top of the ball as you can. Hold the club at the bottom of the grip to give maximum control of the club. You should use the same grip for the short game as you would for the long, although some very good chippers see this part of the game as an extension of the putting stroke and use their putting grip on these shots. Because you are trying to get your eyes as nearly

over the top of the ball as you can and you are gripping the club down at the bottom of the grip, you will bend over the shot more than you would if you were playing a full 5 iron shot. Then, with the weight of your body balanced toward the balls of the feet and with your head over the ball, your stance – the line through the feet, the hips and the shoulders – should be at right angles to the line you are trying to hit along. Your arms should be close to your body and your feet should be close together, no more than 6 inches (15 cm) apart.

You should make sure that the sole of the club lies flat on the ground so that the ball is hit in the direction you want it to go. If the toe of the club is on the ground and the heel of the club off it, the ball would be despatched to the right of the target: conversely, if the heel was on the ground and the toe up in the air, the ball would be pulled to the left of the target.

DEVELOPING A FIRM-WRISTED STROKE

The most important thing about the technique of playing the chip shot is that the wrists must be kept firm throughout the stroke. Place your hands slightly ahead of the ball, as with all the other shots, and then, during the backswing, keep your wrists firm and swing the club low to the ground, using your arms and shoulders. Keep your body as still as possible, moving only to accommodate the slight rock of your shoulders as the club is swung backwards. The through swing should just be as long as the backswing to keep the tempo of the swing smooth. You do not require any wristwork in the swing for a chip shot because the wrists create swing speed and acceleration, and a chip shot does not require great speed, only consistency. Keeping the wrists firm allows you to control the speed of the club-head far more efficiently that if you were to introduce wrist action. The other reason for eliminating wrist action from the shot is that cocking the wrist causes the club to

In the address position for the chip shot the ball is placed opposite the inside of the left heel. The hands are in front of the club-face and the weight favours the left foot (1). The backswing is created by rocking the shoulders to ensure that the stroke is played with the arms, not with the wrists. This method keeps the club-face pointing toward the target (2). At impact, the arms have swung back toward the target, allowing the club-face to dispatch the ball in the intended direction. The body has been kept perfectly still throughout (3).

RIGHT: *Viewed from behind, the address position shows the head over the ball and the body bent forward more because the club has been held short (1). At the top of the backswing, the club has been swung directly away from the target by the arms while the body is kept perfectly still (2). Because the weight is on the left foot at address, the club will be slightly on the downswing when it catches the ball before the turf (3). The head will have remained in the same position throughout the stroke, which allows the club to swing toward the hole (4).*

LEFT: *The length of the follow-through is the same as the length of the backswing. The head and body have remained still as the arms have swung through.*

INSET: *Because the stroke has been played with the arms, the hands and club do not turn over in the follow-through.*

The trajectory of shots toward the flag will be governed by the loft of the club used. The chip shot produces a low trajectory with maximum roll. The pitch and run produces a higher trajectory with a matching amount of roll. The pitch shot produces maximum trajectory, which causes the ball to drop so steeply that there is little or no forward momentum when it lands.

swing in quite a sharp arc, and the club-head would come up off the ground in the backswing, making it very easy, if the downswing were slightly mis-timed, to hit the shot inaccurately. A wristless stroke keeps the club at ground level far longer.

If you are attempting a chip shot from just off the edge of the green, try to duplicate your putting stroke as nearly as you can because it is far easier to judge distance and line when you are thinking of the shot in terms of the putt than it is to try to produce the same shot by thinking of it as some sort of low percentage of your full swing.

When you are playing a chip shot, the ball should be played from the middle of your stance. This makes it easier for you to keep your hands high ahead of the ball at address and at impact.

SELECTING A CLUB

The clubs used for the shot should be selected to keep the ball in the air long enough to make sure it lands on the smooth cut of the green. Generally, the clubs with straighter faces are more likely to do an efficient job of rolling the ball accurately. A shot that lands on the fringe of the green might bounce anywhere. Do not try to scoop the ball up into the air, for the loft on the club will do that if you allow it to swing through the ball.

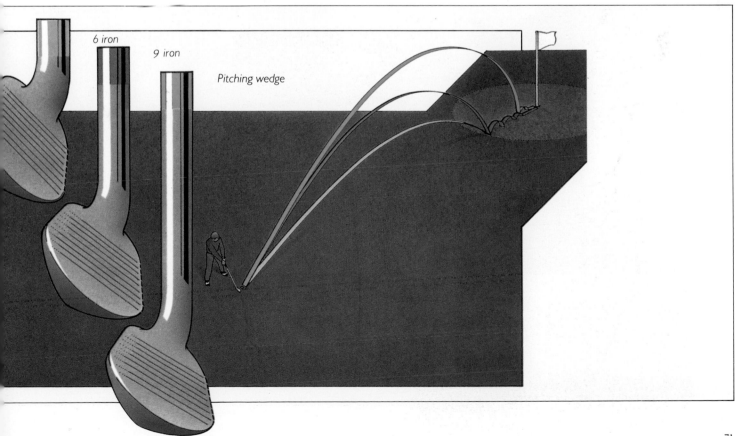

6 iron

9 iron

Pitching wedge

THE PITCH-AND-RUN SHOT

A pitch-and-run shot requires almost the same technique as the chip. The difference is that the ball would be further back from the green, probably between 5 and 20 yards (4 and 18m) further back, and the clubs used would be the 7, 8 or 9 iron. The stance would be a little wider and again the head should be as near over the ball as it could possibly be placed. The hands should be close to the body for control, and the weight should be evenly balanced on both feet. The ball is played in the centre of the stance, and again the shot is played just with the arms and shoulders: the wrists are not used. The backswing would be a little longer, probably going back to between knee and hip height, and the follow-through should be the same length as the backswing because you do not want to hit at the ball quickly or jab at it. It is important to keep the tempo of the swing smooth. The extra loft on the 7, 8 and 9 irons means that the trajectory of the ball will be higher.

TOP ROW: *In the address position, the hands are ahead of the ball, the weight favours the left foot and the head is behind the ball (1).*
The club has been swung straight back from the ball and away from the target using just the arms. The backswing is generous because sudden acceleration, which creates back-spin, is not needed on this shot (2).
Body movement has been kept to a minimum (3).
The club has continued to swing toward the target with the hands continuing to lead the club-face (4).

BOTTOM ROW: *Viewed from behind, the hands are close to the body to allow the head to be over the ball. This makes lining up the shot considerably easier (1).*
Because the arms swing back without any wrist action, the club-face can be kept pointing toward the target, which will guarantee a straight shot as long as the body is kept still (2).
At impact, the position of the body reflects the address position (3). The club continues to swing through the ball toward the target, pulling the right shoulder underneath the stationary head. It is vital that the follow-through should be at least as long as the backswing (4).

THE PITCH SHOT

If you use the same method for the chip and the pitch-and-run shots but play with a pitching wedge or a sand wedge, you will have a pitch shot. A pitch shot climbs steeply into the air, drops almost vertically on to the green with backspin and settles near to the point where it lands. The shot is played with just the arms and shoulder; the wrists are not used. You will find that the maximum distance for this shot without any wrist action is around 40–50 yards (35–45 m). When you come to want to hit the ball further than this, you have to introduce some wrist action to get the club-head swinging more quickly; wrist action should not be introduced into the shot until you are swinging at maximum length with your arms and shoulders. This will be at a point where your hands are swinging up to about shoulder height.

When you are playing an ordinary pitch shot it is vital that the follow-through be at least as long as the backswing, because the follow-through allows the club to use its natural loft to get the ball up into the air. The stance should alter slightly and become slightly open: a line through the feet will point to the left of the target. This is to encourage you to slice slightly across the ball to make the ball fly higher and spin a little more. The last thing you want when you are playing the wedges is a pull or a hook. A slightly open stance allows the club to be swung a little way outside the target line in the takeaway and across that same target line in the downswing, which imparts a slight left-to-right spin on the ball and helps to make the ball climb and land more softly.

THE 60 DEGREE WEDGE

An important addition to the modern short game has been the introduction of the 60 degree wedge, which should be played in exactly the same way as the others – that is with arm and shoulder, not wrist action. This club has come into use because the modern professionals have evolved a method that includes only arm and shoulder action in their short game swing. If you try to play a 60 degree wedge and flick your wrists, you will hit underneath the ball, and will never get the ball to travel a consistent distance because the angle is just too great. Played with no wrist action, the loft of the club can be used effectively both from the fairway and out of the rough and out of bunkers. This club has so much loft on it that to open the club-face and increase that loft makes it impossible to move the ball forward.

Many amateurs watch the professionals on television playing pitch shots that spin the ball back huge distances on the green, and they wonder how they can add this hot to their own game. In fact, the professionals do nothing different from the amateurs: they just do it better. They strike the ball more solidly with the pitching clubs, swing the clubs forward to strike the bottom of the ball and allow the natural loft of the club to spin the ball up in the air. It is the quality of the strike that produces this back-spin, not a trick that the professional keeps up his sleeve. To produce this back-spin the hands must be ahead of the ball at impact and the club must be accelerating into the ball.

Even the professionals get this sort of back-spin only when they are playing a reasonably full shot. They cannot produce it if they are not hitting the ball hard. Many amateurs try to play shots from 20 or 30 yards (18 or 27 m) and expect to get the same amount of back-spin that the professionals get when they are hitting the ball 80 or 90 yards (70 or 80 m). It is important to remember that if you use a shot that produces so much back-spin, you must pitch the ball behind the hole for it to finish close to the hole. This makes courses that are already far too long for the average amateur play even longer. It is much more sensible for amateurs to play a pitch shot that they know will settle or perhaps run a few feet forward rather than try to dig the ball in and make it spin back all the time.

(1) At address the most important thing is to have the hands ahead of the ball so that it can be struck a downward blow.
(2) At the top of the backswing, less weight is transferred on to the right foot because the backswing has been made by swinging the arms up.

(3) Although the weight is on the left side, the head is still behind the ball.
(4) At the end of the swing the club-face has deliberately been held open in order to give the shot maximum height.

When the ball hits the green from a pitch shot it usually leaves an indentation known as a 'ball mark' in the green. It is common courtesy, and within the rules of the game, to repair the damage.

BUNKER SHOTS

It is every golfer's intention when out on the course to avoid, wherever possible, the many problem areas that are strategically placed to add complexity to the holes. Inevitably, however, you will find yourself trapped in one every so often and the problem then is how to escape. Bunkers are certainly not the friendliest of hazards and special techniques are required to get the ball safely out of the sand.

How you go about this will depend to a large extent on the lie of the ball in the sand. Sometimes you may be fortunate enough to find that it has ended up on top of the sand. In this situation you should be able to play a splash shot to get it back onto the fairway or up to the green. Depending on how soft the sand is and how hard the ball has dropped into it, you may be faced with the situation where the ball has partly buried itself. In this case, the problem of removing it is that much more difficult. Harder still, however, is when this situation is combined with the fact that the ball has landed on a slope in the bunker.

There is, however, a special iron to help you come with the specific problems of hitting out of the sand. The design of the sand iron, which has the greatest angle of loft of all the clubs in the set and also a wider base than normal, offers you a great deal of assistance. But much also depends on how well you can adjust your normal techniques and how accurately you can strike the ball.

The ability to swing confidently through the ball, while maintaining an open clubface, is the key to a successful bunker shot.

You can cover comparatively long distances from the fairway bunkers, provided that the ball is well away from the face of the bunker. Nevertheless, there is always the fear of making contact with the sand before the ball, so overly ambitious long carries should never be attempted.

ON THE LEVEL

Where the ball is sitting on top of the sand, several changes are needed from the methods you would use to play a normal shot with a lofted club. Instead of attempting to make contact directly with the face of the ball, you have to aim the point of strike a fraction behind the ball. The result is that you have a small cushion of sand between the club-head and the ball at the point of impact.

Because you want to get maximum lift on the ball, you have to hit across it rather than straight through it. This is done by positioning the ball forward in the stance and aiming the line of the feet and the shoulders off to the left. To play the shot you must swing back and then through as fully as you can, being aware that the swinging arc is upright. This is to ensure that the ball lifts. The speed at which you bring the club down will determine how far forward the ball will go.

When playing out of a fairway – as opposed to greenside – bunker, you will oviously be hoping for reasonable length and should therefore bring the club through fairly quickly. However, you must make sure that the pace remains constant through the swing, since if you speed up the swing part-way though you are almost certain to mis-direct the ball.

When playing out of a deep bunker along-side the green, you will want much more height and very little length in the shot. Therefore you must swing the club more slowly. Another way of softening the flight is to have the ball extremely well forward in the stance – which should be turned left even more – and to open the face of the club-head. You need not worry too much about the ball running on after it lands on the green. In fact, the small cushion of sand is just as capable of putting back-spin on the ball as the club-head is.

It is important to remember that you must never be too ambitious with a shot out of a bunker. If you pay too much attention to sending the ball as far as possible, you may well end up mis-hitting it and quite probably leaving it in the bunker. The golden rule, however the ball is placed in the bunker, is to get it out. Concern about the length of the shot must always come second.

Unlike the procedure for deep greenside bunkers, it is best not to bury your feet in the sand, since this encourages contact with the sand before the ball. It is advisable to hold the club down the handle a little, which firms up the wrist action and ensures a clean contact.

If the ball is partly buried in the sand, you will have to force it out. In order to strike well down to the bottom of the ball, the club-head needs to be swung into the sand before it makes contact. How far before will depend on how deep the ball is lying. What you should be aiming for is to strike the ball as the club-head reaches the lowest point of the swing, and this is something you will have to judge for yourself.

Because you are swinging into the sand, you need to lower yourself slightly into it as well. To achieve this, you just have to shuffle your feet about until they sink in. In this way you should guarantee striking the ball low down. If you do not sink your feet into the sand, you are likely to hit over the top of the ball.

When you take up your stance for this shot, stand square on to the target line and have the ball positioned in the centre of the stance. You will need a strong, full swing into the ball to get it out. You cannot hope for much control over the ball, which is unlikely to lift very high and will tend to run on some way after landing. This is because there will be little or no back-spin on the ball.

The simplest way to hit the ball when it is lying on wet sand is to adopt the techniques for playing a pitch shot. In fact, you may find it easier to use a pitching wedge rather than a sand iron in these circumstances. You should aim to hit the sand just before the ball. The ball will fly lower, unless you can keep the club-face open, and you will have little control over the forward momentum once it lands.

LEFT: *This sequence illustrates a perfect splash shot out of the bunker. The club-head, which is kept open throughout, travels across the target line from out to in, catching the sand before the ball.*

OPPOSITE, TOP ROW: *To play a splash shot, address the ball with the blade lying slightly open. Since the stance is open, the club will travel across the ball, helping to weaken its forward flight, yet increasing its lift.*

OPPOSITE, LEFT: *When the ball is plugged in the sand, you need to take up a square stance. Line the club-head up square with the ball in a central position, and hit through the sand (opposite, right).*

ON A SLOPE

When you have to play up the slope of a bunker, you have the same problems as on a grass slope but with the added complication that there is sand to contend with.

You cannot play the basic splash shot here since there would be no cushion of sand between the club-head and the ball. The best way to overcome this problem is to lean with the slope so that, in effect, you are playing the shot on flat ground. This allows you to create that cushion of sand you need.

Similar problems exist when you have to play down the slope of a bunker, although here the trouble is that you often bury the club-head in the sand too early. The result is that when it reaches the ball it strikes too high up. The solution is to lean as much with the slope as possible, use a very steep swing and come down firmly just behind the ball, which you should have well back in the stance. The best you can really hope for is for the ball to fly out of the bunker. You will not get any height on the ball and without back-spin you will not be able to control its forward momentum once it has landed.

The danger with this type of shot is that the blade of the club will make contact with the ball too cleanly. The correct procedure is to lean your body with the slope (above left) so that it is possible to take some sand before you strike the ball, but at the same time avoid burying the club-head in the slope (left).

OPPOSITE: *Although it may appear to be quite simple, a bunker shot from an uphill slope is one that even professionals dislike.*

RIGHT: *By far the most difficult bunker shot is that where the ball lies on a down slope. Although it is very difficult to lean with the slope, every effort should be made to do so.*

OPPOSITE TOP: *Pick the club up very sharply on the back swing so that you can make an unnaturally steep delivery across the ball.*

OPPOSITE, BOTTOM: *Through long hours of practice as a young man, Gary Player made himself one of the finest bunker players in the world. Because he lacked the power of some of his contemporaries, he knew he would be hitting longer clubs to the green which would mean that he would miss more greens. So he taught himself to recover from bunkers in order to compete with his more powerful rivals. He became so good at recovery shots, it is said that on holes with difficult greens, Player would aim his second shot into the sand bunkers because he was more confident of getting his bunker shot close to the hole than he was a long putt. Player's ability to win in countries all over the world is in no small part due to his excellence when playing from sand. He is a great competitor who never gives up and this is typified in his attitude toward playing recovery shots.*

PUTTING

There have been numerous designs of putters over the years – even one with a shaft that entered the head vertically and allowed you to swing it between your legs, as if you were playing croquet. (This type, incidentally, has long since been outlawed.) Nowadays putters are generally upright, with the shaft entering the head at a slight angle.

Because of the type of club being used and the nature of the shot, the technique involved on the putting green is, of course, very different from that used on other parts of the course. Control is vital, since the shot needs to have exactly the right amount of pace and be deadly accurate. And, unlike any other shots on the course, the putt is played along the ground, which is why there is little or no angle of loft on the club-face.

As with any other shot on the golf course, working out the line of the shot and aiming correctly is all-important and on these will depend where you take up your stance. However, it is possible to work on the basic techniques of the putting stroke without taking precise aim and these aspects are therefore being looked at first.

STANCE

You must make sure when you set up for the putt that you keep everything squarely in line with the direction of your aim, which as you will see later is not always directly to the hole. This means that your feet, which are only about six inches (15 cm) apart, hips, arms and shoulders must be lined up parallel to the target line. The body should be bent forward over the putter which, when the stroke is played, should be travelling in the same line as that of the ball toward the target. You should be able to move the putter backward and forward comfortably and smoothly, close to the ground.

There is a tendency for learners to lean too far over the shot and this can be as bad as standing too upright. The effect of either of these two faults is to force the shoulders out of line when you apply the correct grip.

BALL POSITION

When preparing for the putt, you must make sure that the ball is positioned well forward in your stance. In fact, it should be roughly level with the inside of your left foot.

The width of the stance when putting should never be more than (9 in [23 cm]) and the ball should always be played from a point just opposite the left foot.

There can be no better advice on putting than to have everything square to the line of the shot. Common sense will tell you that if the shoulders, forearms, legs and feet are all parallel to the route along which the ball must travel, then it has to be easier to roll that ball truly toward the target. The standard, professional method of putting is well demonstrated here. One very important feature is that the eyes are directly over the ball.

GRIP

The grip used for putting is markedly different to that used for the other clubs. The handle should *not* cross the palm but rather pass just under the bottom of the left thumb, with the hand 'laid off' so that the top of the handle is visible.

The left thumb should be on the top of the handle rather than to the side, and both this and the thumb of the right hand must point directly down the handle. With this arrangement you will ensure that the left wrist stays well forward. The same rule as before applies when taking up the grip on the putter, with the handle placed in the left hand before adding the right.

The putter should be gripped firmly, but never tightly. Many great putters concede that they grip the club very lightly. If you grip the club too firmly, the muscles in the forearms tense, and it becomes hard to transmit any sort of feel from the putter face back up into the body of the brain. Also, making a smooth stroke is easier if the muscles are relaxed.

Putting demands a very delicate stroke and so requires the greatest sensitivity in the hands and fingers. If you grip the club tightly it will inhibit this sensitivity. Good feel allows the golfer to respond to different textures of green or general putting conditions – putting in the rain, putting in the wind, putting down or up hill or putting on different grasses, for example.

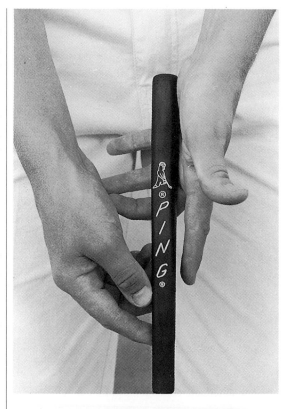

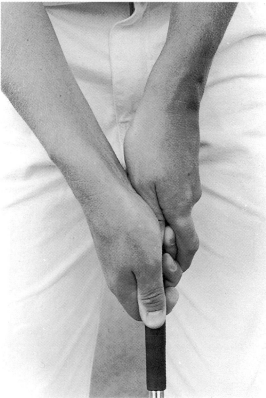

Since the putter is the one club in the bag that is used as near to the perpendicular as it is possible to get in golf, the grip changes from the traditional Vardon style to one where the thumbs are directly down the handle. The handle of the club passes comfortably up through the palm of the hands rather than in the fingers.

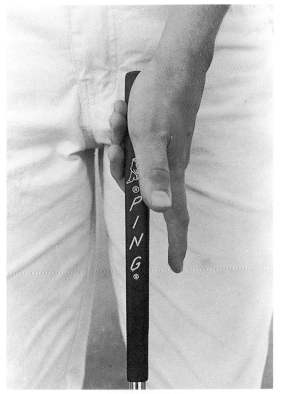

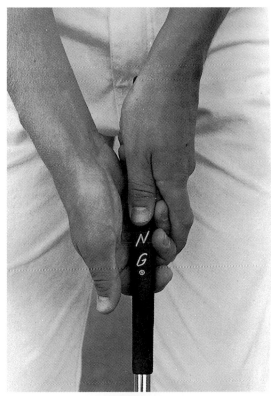

Overlapping or interlocking are down to personal preference. Here a reverse overlap is used, where two fingers of the right hand are covered by the forefinger of the left.

THE PUTT

Unlike all the other shots in golf, with the exception of the tiny chip-and-run shots, there should be minimal movement of the body when striking the ball on the green. Apart from the gentle to and fro swing of the arms and a slight rocking movement of the shoulders, the rest of your body should remain perfectly still – and particularly your head. Obviously you will move this in order to look up and down the line of the shot prior to hitting the ball, but once you are satisfied with your aim and have decided what strength to put into the stroke, your head should come down to look at the ball and remain there until well after you have stroked the ball towards the hole.

How you apply pace to the ball is, to a large extent, a matter of personal taste. There are two methods you can adopt. One is to maintain the same length of stroke (the total distance the putter travels back then forth along the target line) whether it is a short putt you are playing or a long one. The extra pace is applied by striking the ball harder.

The second method is to maintain a standard tempo throughout the putting stroke, regardless of the length of shot required. Players who prefer to do this then lengthen the stroke accordingly for the longer putts (by drawing the putter back then sending it further through) and similarly reduce it for the shorter putts.

OPPOSITE: *One of the secrets of successful putting is to take the putter head back and through the ball with as smooth, short and low to the ground a movement as possible, as shown here from a front and side view*

LEFT: *The nature of the putting grip tends to stifle wrist action rather than encourage it and this is ideal for the putting stroke, which comes more from a forearm and hand motion rather than a wrist and hand action.*

Since it is almost impossible to find a putting green that is flat – not that any would be designed that way – it is necessary to learn how to 'read' the green. The rolling ball will be affected by gravity and will therefore turn from the high side to the low side of any slope. Judging how high to the right or left to send the ball is known as 'taking the borrow', a key factor in successful putting.

LINING UP THE PUTT

Apart from adopting the right putting technique, it is also crucial to the success of the shot that you can line up the putt accurately by deciding how the green slopes and therefore where to aim the ball. Unfortunately it is rarely as simple as just aiming for the flag. Aspects that should always be given careful consideration include the grass itself – whether, for example, it is thick or close-cut, fine or coarse, damp or dry. Also relevant is how the green itself runs, whether it slopes up or down, or equally off to left or the right.

Since there can be no margin for error if you are attempting to hole out in as few putts as possible, you must also take into account the natural elements – and, in particular, the strength and direction of any wind that is blowing on the green.

Incidentally, before you get down on your hands and knees and start pulling the turf about, you should remember that testing the green itself is against the rules even with a club-head. So all your investigations must be carried out with the eyes alone.

Needless to say, the drier and closer-cut the green, the faster the ball will run across it. Conversely, the damper and thicker it is, the slower the ball will travel. The stronger you play the shot, therefore, the less likely it is to be affected by the surface of the green – over reasonably short distances, at any rate.

SLOPING GREENS

The trouble with any slope, of course, is that if you play the ball along the ground it will be carried with the slope. If you do not make any adjustment when lining up the shot, the ball will fall agonizingly away from the target line instead of running straight to the hole. To compensate for this, you must therefore aim your putt up the slope first at just the right spot and pace so that the ball will then run down with the slope into or close to the hole. This is known as 'taking the borrow'.

Working out how much a green slopes and, therefore, where exactly to aim the ball so as to bring it back to the hole is not the easiest of tasks

LEFT: *A tiny putt still counts as much as a massive drive, and it can prove very costly should one careless moment where concentration lapses be allowed to creep in . . .*

RIGHT: *The 'plumb-bob' method is a means of using the putter to gauge how much the ground slopes away from the vertical hang of the club. By lining up the lower part of the shaft through the ball and then bringing your eye up the shaft until it is level with the hole, however much the hole is to the right or left, that is the amount you should borrow when playing the putt.*

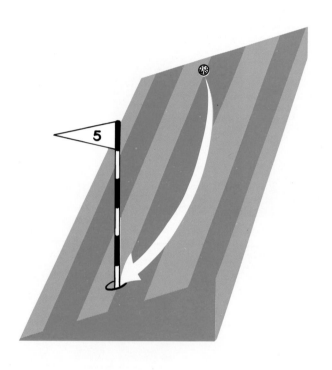

On a sloping green it is essential that you allow enough for the slope and aim the putt so that the ball runs back down with the slope – hopefully into the hole. In such a situation much will depend on your judgement and plenty of practice.

on the golf course. Those with a very good eye and an uncanny knack of judgment may be able to get it right most of the time. But there is no doubt that this skill is somewhat of a gift not granted to every golfer. Fortunately, however, there is a method by which you can calculate fairly accurately the degree of the slope relatively easily and therefore where roughly to aim your ball.

Sometimes called the 'plumb-bob' method, it works on a similar principle to that of the piece of equipment used to establish a true vertical. In the case of golf, the equipment used is the putter. The exercise is best carried out from a crouching position a pace or two from the ball. If this is a problem, then move further back and try it from the upright position. You must take up your position behind the ball so that it is in the line of sight between you and the flag. Then suspend your

putter by holding it lightly near the top of the handle, so that the shaft appears to be directly over the centre of the ball. Make sure you hold the putter so that its head is pointing either toward you or the hole. If not, the shaft will hang at an angle.

Take your eyes up the shaft to the point where it is level with the hole. In the case of a perfectly straight putt, where the ground is not sloping, the shaft will run right through the hole. But if the ground does slope, then this point will be either to the right or to the left of the hole and it is to this point that you should aim your shot.

While this method is quite useful and does offer a reasonable guide, it cannot of course tell you *how much* the green slopes up or down toward the hole or about the condition of the turf. These factors are all relevant in assessing what

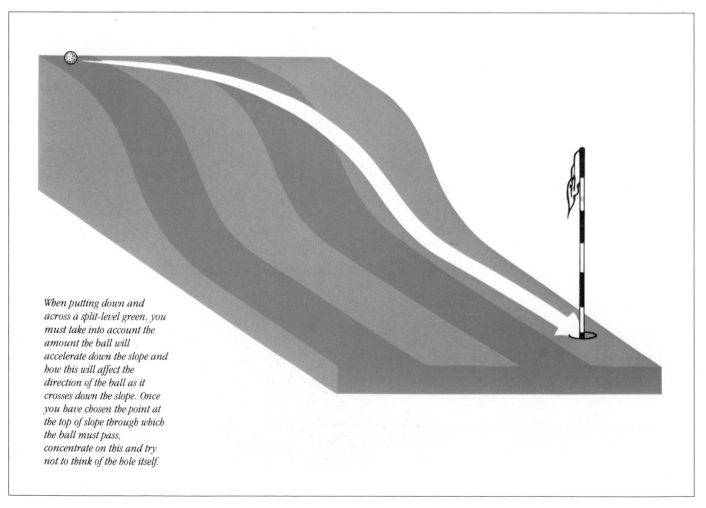

When putting down and across a split-level green, you must take into account the amount the ball will accelerate down the slope and how this will affect the direction of the ball as it crosses down the slope. Once you have chosen the point at the top of slope through which the ball must pass, concentrate on this and try not to think of the hole itself.

pace you need to play the shot.

Where the green runs downhill to the hole as well as sloping to one side, you should take the precaution of increasing the amount of the borrow – that is, aiming to a point even wider than the one indicated by the plumb-bob method. Conversely, where the green runs uphill, you should aim somewhere between the estimated point and the hole.

At the end of the day, working out the slope and other relevant conditions on the green will depend on your experience. The more practice you have playing on different types of green, the more proficient you will be at judging the composition of a green and playing it accurately.

ADVERSE WEATHER

Unfortunately slopes are not the only problem you are likely to encounter when you get to the green. Rain can make quite a difference to the run of the ball, since the wet grass will take much of the pace out of the shot. In this case, you will need to reduce the amount of borrow to compensate since you will have to play a stronger shot.

Strong winds can also play havoc with your calculations, and any allowances you make will depend on whether the wind is blowing down the slow or up it. Where it is with the slope, you will have to increase the borrow, while with the wind blowing against the slope, the effect will be greatly reduced and you will therefore need to allow much less borrow.

SPLIT-LEVEL GREENS

Sloping greens pose one set of problems which you will, with experience, overcome, but further problems await you in the shape of split-level greens. The secret of playing on this type of green is to have a good look at both sections. Check on the slope between each section and get firmly fixed in your mind a marker spot to which and through which you should aim the ball. (Naturally you will have to check as to whether either level of green slopes and take this into account as previously described.)

The easier approach to this type of green is definitely from the lower level up to the higher level. There are several reasons for this. For a start, you should be playing a firmer putt to get the ball up the hill. Also, because the higher section of the green will be nearer to your own eye level, you will find it a lot easier to check the lie of the turn and where the slope may be.

In this situation, you need to fix only one marker point, at the top of the slope on the edge of the higher level. This is because the strength of the shot needed to carry the ball up the hill should, in normal cases, override any problems in the lower level turf. Thus you can concentrate on establishing the correct spot on the top level from which your ball will hopefully run to the hole.

Putting down from the higher level to the lower one is more problematical, since you will not be able to use so much strength in the shot. You must also take into account the conditions of the turf on both levels, particularly since the ball will gain added pace from the steepness of the down slope. It is essential to judge what the ball's reaction will be, both in pace and direction, and estimate the point at which it must roll over the top of the slope. That is the place you must aim for and it should take your mind off the hole itself.

The biggest problem with downhill putts is judging the pace of the shot. If you underhit the ball, it might not even make the slope and you are then faced with a similar problem all over again. Equally, if you hit the shot too hard, the ball will pick up extra pace down the slope and run well past the hole. But, whatever you do, make sure the ball gets onto the lower level, even if it is not as close as you wish to the hole.

Where to look when playing this type of putt is equally crucial. One thing you must not do is be tempted to look at the hole. Having worked out your marker point, concentrate just on this. Go for the marker point and trust your judgment.

Life will be made even more complicated if you have to play up or down a split-level green at an angle. Coping with this is basically a matter of experience. The general rule, however, is to over-estimate the borrow you need and make sure, if you are putting up the slope, that you get the ball onto the higher level. Letting the ball roll back down the hill can prove disastrous.

SPECIALIST SHOTS

The techniques discussed so far will enable you to play the ball straight at a height and distance determined mainly by the type of club you are using. But what makes golf such a fascinating game is the fact that playing it requires a great deal of variety with every single shot. This is because courses are designed to offer challenges and problems. Now you have to learn to control the ball, and how to cope with some of the awkward places it will inevitably reach. This chapter provides details of how to achieve those specialist shots that can get you out of trouble.

AWKWARD LIES

You will be straying soon enough off the straight and narrow fairways of golf. Do not be too disheartened to find yourself with awkward lies. You may have graduated from pitch and putt courses on which the crisp shots and the soaring golf ball gave you an enhanced view of your ability. You may have come from the driving ranges where you found life and power in your hands, which must now be applied in a wholly different situation. Some of the world's top golf courses are designed in undulating countryside which the course architect wished to preserve, as a challenge to your skills and a pleasant sight to your eyes. He aimed to bring out the best in you. It is up to you now to bring out the best aim for him.

When in an awkward lie, do not be too bold, and watch where you position your weight. These cautions should come into your mind when you find your ball in two of the most awkward lies: an uphill or a downhill lie.

DOWNHILL

You look at the target line with the ground flowing away from you in the downhill lie and you feel that on a flat fairway you might need an 8 iron, say, to pitch the ball onto the green. But you are striking down into the ball because of the slope.

Depending on the degree of slope, that position is going to tighten up the loft of the club, giving it the action of a 7 iron or perhaps a 6 iron. It is the same as hooding the club-face over the ball, closing the face, and thus reducing the loft.

Assume a stance where the ball is well back towards the right foot so that you swing directly into it. Take care not to hit the ground first. If you hit the ball first and it goes up and away you will put slice-spin on it, like the back-spin chopshot in table tennis. The ball will go left and come back to the right. If the lie of the ball allows you to reach for a straighter-faced, less lofted, club, because the target is more than a long pitch away, aim further left. The slice-spin should bring it round, if your swing matches your chosen club.

When taking aim, grip the club a little lower than normal – it's called going down the shaft. It will give you more control for this awkward shot. Keep your hands forward of the ball.

You must feel comfortable for this shot, confident that you will not lose your balance as you swing the club-head through the ball. Flex your knees – the right one will be bent inwards a little to balance your weight on the slope. Begin with a short backswing. Take the club back with your arms, not your shoulders, on a line suggested by the slope of the ground. Keeping your head still will bring confidence that you will not lose your balance as you strike downwards and through the ball.

To adjust to a downhill lie, (1) The loft of a club is decreased from an eight to a seven or six, depending on the steepness of the slope.

(2) The ball should be towards the back foot. Your weight is in front of the ball. From this position it is easier to ensure that you strike the ball first and not hit the ground behind the ball.

(3) Restrict body movement by taking only a short backswing, keeping the weight in front of the ball.

(4) Don't try for too much length. Ensure that you keep your balance.

(1) The angle of the club-head is increased. A 7 iron will become an 8 or even a 9 iron, depending on the steepness of the slope.

(2) The ball should be in front of the centre line, enabling you to swing through, with the slope, to achieve maximum lift. The length of the backswing should be determined by the angle of the slope. You must not swing so far back as to lose your balance.

UPHILL

The slope increases the loft of the club so that a 7 iron played on an upward slove will carry the ball the shorter distance of an 8 iron or, on a steeper slope, a 9 iron.

You are swinging into a ball on an uphill slope. This will have the effect of increasing the loft on the club-face. This makes you think twice about club selection. It is not enough to choose a club which will suit the distance. It has to carry enough loft to lift the ball clear of the slope. Boldness is not your friend when you are facing a ball with your left leg and foot higher than the right. The ball must be struck on the upswing. This will cause it to have a hook-spin, so allow for this built-in movement in the flight by aiming off a little to the right.

Facing a steep slope, you will need height to clear it. You will be tempted towards a stronger club to achieve distance. Do not be too greedy: you may catch the slope and lose distance. Watch out, too, for that natural tendency to move your body weight into the slope on the downswing. This troublemaker means your downswing will lose its arc and will come in too steeply, 'de-lofting' the club-face to lower the trajectory of the ball, which will fly into the slope.

Here is how to play the shot. Stand behind the ball and picture the flight. Seek the target line. Remember the ball will move slightly to the left. Do not be tempted to be too bold. Take aim. Grip the club lower down than normal to give you a little more control. Take your stance with the ball positioned more towards the left foot than the right.

Your posture will depend on the steepness of the slope, your left knee bending more than your right, so that your body angle is as near as possible to 90° to the slope. Keep your weight on your right leg so you may sweep through the ball when making the strike. Keep the backswing short to a maximum of a three-quarter swing. Swing through the ball, with a follow-through high enough to ensure that you do not lose your balance.

(1) Take a more upright stance at an angle of 90° to the slope. From this position the swing plane will be flatter than normal.

(2) The swing should be within your balance limits. The longer the swing, the greater the likelihood of loss of balance.

(3) In the follow-through, keep your head still a little longer than usual.

ABOVE THE FEET

Another tricky situation is playing the ball when it is above your feet, on a slope going upwards from left to right. Balance is always the keystone when building a stance for awkward lies.

Flex your knees so that you have your weight solidly over your feet and can feel that it is not going to slip onto your heels. Once again, go down the shaft a little with your grip to gain more control and allow you to stand closer to the ball. Assume a more than normally upright stance at an angle of 90° to the slope. Take the ball from a spot nearer to the left foot than the right.

The swing must be within your balance limits: the longer the swing, the more likely it is that you will sway away from the ball. The stance will give you a flatter swing place and, coupled with the fact that the toe of the club will be slightly off the ground, the club-face will close slightly. This gives the ball draw – moving right to left in flight.

Your stance allows you to take a confident swing because there is no restriction on the body turn. With a maximum three-quarter backswing, concentrate on sweeping the club through the ball to a good high finish.

(1) To anchor your balance at the address, your weight should be on your heels. Stick your bottom out more than usual as you flex your knees. From this position the swing plane will be more upright than normal.

(2) From this position, the hips will not be able to move, so concentrate on generating power from the shoulder turn.

(3) As with shots from all awkward lies, the head should be kept still a little longer than usual to prevent loss of balance.

BELOW THE FEET

When the ball is below the feet, that is on a slope rising from right to left, it presents the most awkward of the four lies discussed here. The amount of slope will determine the distance that you stand from the ball.

To anchor your balance, keep your weight back on your heels as you address the ball. Stick your bottom out a little more than usual as you flex your knees. You can feel immediately that this position will restrict the amount of shoulder and body turn in the swing and will encourage a steeper than normal swing plane.

Your balance is threatened in this shot. You have no shoulder turn to help your swing. You must leave that to your arms and hands. Spread your feet to provide the best chance of balancing confidently.

Aim down to the left of the target. This will help you to keep the club-head square. Take your stance so that the ball lies in the middle of your feet, and grip the club at the top end of the grip, because for this stroke you need to use as much of the shaft as you can.

Let your arms and hands control the swing without affecting your balance.

THE DRAW AND FADE

The two most commonly shaped shots – that is, shots that are deliberately bent in one direction or the other by the golfer – are known as the draw and the fade. The draw is a shot that starts slightly to the right of target and that bends to the left. The fade is the opposite: it starts slightly to the left of the target and bends to the right.

The ability to bend the ball is a skill that has been developed by all the greater players. The main reasons for acquiring this skill are to manoeuvre the ball around obstacles and to negate the effect of cross-winds. A shot that bends from right to left is known as a draw; a shot that bends from left to right is a fade. Most good players base their game on one or the other of these two shot patterns.

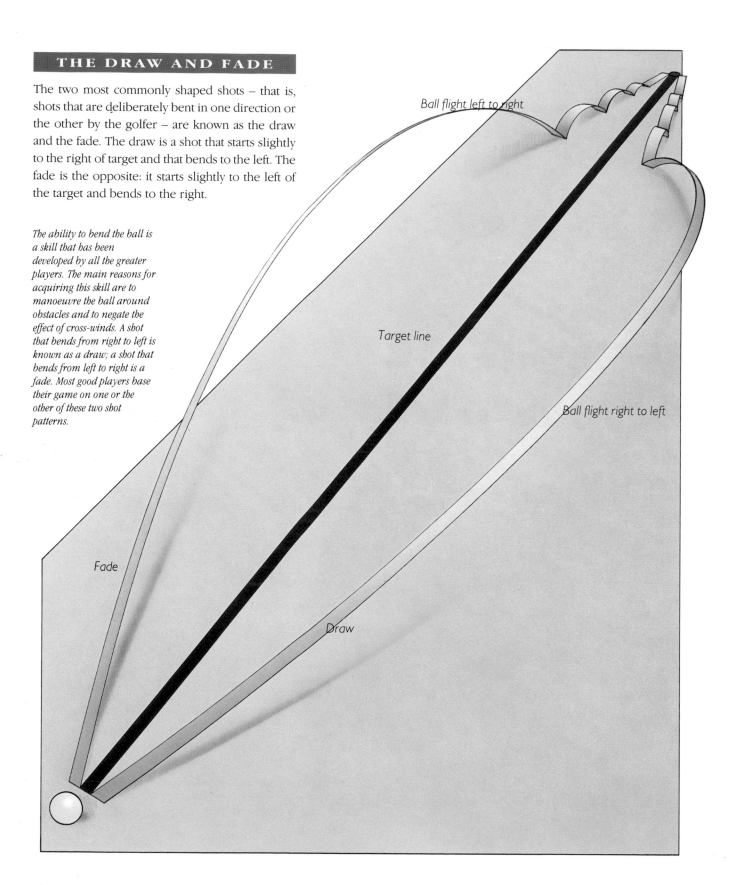

Ball flight left to right

Target line

Ball flight right to left

Fade

Draw

THE DRAW

To develop the draw, set up as if you were playing a straight shot but aim to the right of your target leaving the club-face aimed straight at the target. If you swing normally along the line that you have set up – that is, to the right of the target – the club-face will be closed to this line at impact, and a hook spin will be applied to the ball, making it curve from right to left in the air.

The trajectory of the ball will be lower than normal, and the ball will travel farther. Most of this extra distance will be roll after the ball has landed; so when you play a drawn or hooked shot, it is important to remember to use less club than you would normally require for a straight shot, for example.

It is not necessary to change the basic swing to draw the ball from right to left. The only adjustments required are that the player aims the body and swings to the right of the target while aiming the club-face directly toward the target. Aiming to the right in this manner effectively moves the ball toward the right foot in the stance.

TOP ROW: *Viewed from behind, it is clear that the club-head swings further inside the target line than it would do from a square stance (2). At the top of the backswing the club is deeper – that is, more behind the player – than it would be when a straight shot is played (3). Because the club is approaching the ball from further inside the target line, the arms and hands have to rotate more to square up the club-face (4). It is this rotation that applies the anti-clockwise spin to the ball (5).*

BOTTOM ROW: *Because the club is moving further inside the target line, the shoulders are pulled further around in the backswing and a stronger, deeper position is achieved at the top (2) and (3). From halfway down, extra hand and arm rotation is necessary to square up the face at impact. The head and upper body must be kept behind the ball (4) and (5).*

LEFT: *Through the ball, the hands and arms have rotated sufficiently to impart right-to-left spin on the ball (6) and (6).*

RIGHT: *The extra rotation of the hands and arms pulls the club into a flatter plane at the finish of the swing. This is shown by the position of the hands at the end of the follow-through: they will be around the left shoulder rather than above it (7) and (7).*

To prepare for the fade shot, the body is aimed to the left of the target following the line along which the ball is required to start. The club-face is pointed toward the target. Opening the stance in this fashion has the effect of moving the ball toward the left foot (1) and (1).

THE FADE

To fade the ball aim to the left of the target along the line on which you wish to start the shot and open the club-face to aim it at the target. The club is still swung in the normal way along the line of the set up – that is, left of target – but the open club-face will produce a slicing blow at impact that will make the ball curve left to right in flight. The effective loft of the club is increased because the club-face is open to the line of swing, making sliced shots rise higher and travel shorter dis-

tances. Remember, therefore, that when trying to fade the ball, use more club.

Two of the most successful players in the history of the game. Ben Hogan and Lee Trevino, adopted the fade as their standard shot pattern. This type of shot is a combination of left-to-right spin and back-spin, which exhausts the ball's energy during its upward climb. The ball then drops softly on the ground, eliminating the unpredictable roll that is a product of the draw and allowing great accuracy of placement.

LOW AND HIGH SHOTS

Low shots require some slight alterations in the address position. First, play the ball further back in the centre of the stance, which should be a little wider than normal; second, hold the club toward the bottom of the grip; and third, place more weight on the left leg. Your hands should be well in front of the ball at address. The wider stance and the weight on the left side will help to keep the backswing shorter than normal, and the ball should be hit with a punching action, which curtails the follow-through. When you are hitting a lot shot, take more club than you need, because you do not want the ball to spin too much as this will make it climb and defeat your objective.

To hit the ball high also requires several changes in the address position. Take up a slightly narrower stance, with the ball position just inside the left heel, and hold the club at the very top of the grip. These changes make it easier to achieve a long backswing and an even longer follow-through. Make sure that the head is kept well behind the shot all the way through the swing, and remember than an open club-face will help you to get the ball up quickly.

RIGHT: *Many professionals claim it is more necessary to have the skill deliberately to hit the ball high or low than it is to be able to draw or fade the ball. The high shot is useful when you have to play over banks or trees; the low shot is vital if you want to keep the ball under the wind or under low-hanging tree branches. Another reason for hitting the ball high is to stop it quickly on the greens, whereas on fast-running, hard courses the low running shot is sometimes the only one that can be played.*

High

Low

Target line

ABOVE: *At address for the low shot, the ball should be played further back in the stance, the weight should favour the left foot, and the hands should hold the club at the bottom of the grip (inset) and be kept ahead of the blade of the club.*

ABOVE: *At address for the high shot, the ball should be played further forward in the stance, with the weight favouring the right foot. The club should be held at the very top of the grip (inset) and the hands are directly behind the club-face at address.*

In playing both low and high shots it is important to remember that the length of swing is the dominating factor in the trajectory of the ball. The short punch swing makes the ball fly low because the acceleration of the club-head occurs only over a short distance; therefore, all the energy is exploded into the back of the ball. The long swing has a more even tempo, and the acceleration is spread over a greater arc: therefore, because the club-face is not accelerating as quickly, the club is allowed to run under the ball much more and the high follow-through helps to keep the arc shallow and lift it high into the air avoiding the hazard.

PLAYING FROM A DIVOT

One of the most frustrating circumstances in golf is to hit a perfect tee shot only to find that it has finished in a divot hole in the middle of a fairway. This 'rub of the green' can be extremely irritating, but, if you use a little common sense, it need not cost you any shots. If the ball is in the back of the divot hole, it is not such a serious problem. Make your normal swing, trying not to hit at the ball, and make sure you follow-through. The worst thing that could happen is that you may catch the ball thin – that is, not quite at the bottom – and it will fly lower and roll further than you anticipated. Even so, it should finish in your target area. If you try to dig the ball out by chopping down on it, you considerably increase the possibility of error, and your worst shot will be a 'fat' one, which will go no distance at all.

The shot from the middle of the divot is played as nearly as possible to a normal shot, but with the emphasis once again on the follow through. This helps to make the ball fly and eliminates the chop from the swing which would be disastrous in this situation.

The first thing to do when the ball is in the front of the divot is to recognize that it will limit your ability to achieve distance. Once you decide how far you can hit the shot, take the most lofted club that will produce that distance, then swing down and through the ball making sure that your hands are ahead of the blade at impact.

When the ball lies in a divot hole, the address position is exactly the same as it would be for a normal shot. No compensations are required, because a normal swing provides the best chance for a successful recovery.

PLAYING OUT OF ROUGH

If your ball lies in heavy rough you may have a problem when the long grass wraps itself around the shaft of the club on both the back and down-swings, making it difficult to control the alignment of the clubface. The best way to deal with this is to address the ball with the club above the grass and the face slightly open. Then lift the club as straight upwards as you can and drop it down slightly behind the ball as you would if you were playing a sand shot. Do not try to follow through. Let the sole of the club slide under the ball and pop it straight up into the air through the grass.

The steep angle of descent will reduce the amount of grass that can wrap itself around the

BELOW: (1) When playing from heavy rough, the ball should be positioned back toward the right foot in the stance because this is the one occasion in golf when a wide, shallow swing will not be effective. (2) The club is lifted straight up in the air on the backswing. There is no shoulder or hip turn, and the weight is kept equally balanced on both feet. The feeling of the backswing is definitely a 'lift' of the club and not a swing.

shaft and prevent the face from closing too much. Grass tends to wrap itself around the hosel and shaft of the club which slows it down, but it does not slow down the toe of the club, which keeps going quickly and turns over into a closed position. When you are playing out of rough there is always a chance that the ball will fly to the left of where you aimed. It will also fly lower with a closed club-face and have more roll on it than a normal shot; so remember to allow for this when you are setting up the shot. You should also remember that the grass in the rough will come between the club-face and the ball when you strike the ball, and in so doing eliminate the chance of any back-spin. This is another reason why the ball will fly lower and roll more when it lands.

BELOW: *(3) and (4) The downswing is just a steep chop with the arms aimed at striking rough 1 inch (2.5 cm) behind the ball. If any attempt were made to sweep the ball out of long rough, the grass would wrap itself around the shaft of the club, slowing it down and turning the club-face over.*

LEFT: *(5) No attempt should be made to follow through because the direction of the stroke has been so steeply downward.*

BELOW: *Arnold Palmer, whose tremendous physical strength makes light of heavy rough, pitches from deep rough. Note how the rough has stopped the club from following through, although Palmer has been able to force the club through on to the ball.*

PLAYING WITH SPIN

In an ideal world the golf club would travel true into the back of every ball and the loft, according to the club being used, would impart only one kind of spin – back-spin. The ball would travel directly on target, soaring to the appropriate height and landing dead on target.

However, golfers are not machines and golf courses are uneven places exposed to all sorts of conditions, and almost every shot played on them is an original one. Therefore another type of spin is created, whether out of choice or by accident, often violent in its extent. It is called side-spin.

Moving a ball so that it turns off its original course can, when done accidentally, be soul-destroying. But when it is applied intentionally it is a most rewarding and stroke-saving ability. There is, therefore, a great advantage to be had in possessing the skill that can turn a ball in flight. You can fight the wind or choose to use it, and you can avoid hazards or curve the ball around them.

The two basic types that golfers use are back-spin and side-spin. The first is the easier and more obvious to apply, since by striking the ball accurately and cleanly the job is done. Because of the way club-faces are angled, particularly the more lofted ones, and the fact that the best place to strike the ball is just below centre, you have already achieved your objective.

Although the height given by back-spin does not alter the direction of the ball, the effect it has when the ball lands is invaluable. On impact with the ground, the ball should either stop dead or depending on the amount of spin applied, roll back a short way. This type of control can be crucial. Side-spin is a lot harder to apply, since you have to not only alter the swing path of the club but also to strike the ball with the club-face off square.

Side-spin takes one of two forms. Either you can hit the ball off to the left in such a way that as the spin takes effect the ball comes back into line, or you can hit it off to the right and then bring it back in from that direction. The first type of spin, depending on how great an arc you send the ball along the shot, is described as drifting from a 'fade' to a 'slice' in extreme cases. When playing the ball out to the right with gentle spin this is described as a 'draw' shot, while with extreme spin the shot is a 'hook'.

BACK-SPIN

The timing and accuracy of your swing direction is crucial to the imparting of back-spin. As already mentioned, because of the degree of loft built in to the face of the clubs, you only have to hit the ball cleanly and squarely with a lofted club to impart back-spin. Obviously, the more lofted the club, the greater the back-spin. So, whereas with the 1 iron you will get maximum distance for an iron shot but minimum lift and spin, with the loftiest iron – the sand iron – you will achieve maximum height and spin, but little distance.

However, there is a further way of increasing the back-spin on the ball, which you will need to master if you want this type of control on longer shots where you will be using clubs with less loft. It involves delaying the uncocking of the wrists until very late in the down swing so that the ball is struck with a more descending blow. The base of the swing is moved beyond the ball so that your club-head strikes the ball and then, after an inch or so, the ground. You can also achieve this by putting more of your weight onto the left side of your body as you swing down. This is a fairly advanced skill, which is best used by experienced players.

There are obviously times when you will not want so much back-spin on the ball. The most common situation is from the tee, when normally you want your drive to run on as far as possible. Fortunately there is no real problem here, since the driver has a minimum degree of loft in the club-head.

Choosing a club with less loft is, in fact, the simplest method of reducing back-spin. When using a club with less loft than normal, move your grip down the club-handle so that you are holding the club as though it were a shorter, more lofted pitching club. Then position yourself so that the ball is slightly further back in the stance than it should be for the type of club you are using. There will be occasions when you may decide to use this technique to ensure plenty of run on the ball.

Golf is rarely a straightforward game and it is therefore essential to understand how to play a variety of spin shots in order to avoid trouble – or at least extricate yourself from it when necessary.

There is another way of emphasizing the reduction of back-spin on the ball, and that is to keep the movement of your hands and wrists to a minimum during the through swing, since activity in this area always encourages spin on the ball.

In general middle irons (numbers 5, 6 and 7) with their extra loft on the club-face, supply increased back-spin which will help you check the ball from running on too far, making them ideal for shots to the green. However, you must be comfortably within range of the club you select so that you are not tempted to force the shot. When in doubt, use a slightly less lofted club to ensure that you make the distance to the target.

The sand iron has a key advantage near the green as it generates very heavy back-spin and can help you clear an obstacle in the way of your shot. If you need back-spin on a bunker shot, don't worry: the small cushion of sand is just as capable of putting back-spin on the ball as the club-head is.

RIGHT: *The spin everyone searches for initially is back-spin, which is the true spin of a ball struck directly from a perfect swing plane and on an accurate swing path. The result is that the control put on the ball can bring it to a very abrupt halt when it lands.*

One problem when a ball with back-spin lands is that it can leave a nasty pitchmark, which should be repaired. But this mark is the sign of quality in the strike. The fact that the ball was still turning quite violently backward when it struck the ground shows how effective the contact of the blade of the club on the ball was in the first place.

RIGHT: *In order to turn the ball in the air from left to right, it is essential that the club travels through the ball from outside to in, bearing in mind that the face of the club should be kept open from that swing path.*

SIDE-SPIN

The determining factor in applying side-spin to the ball so that during its flight it alters direction – either to the left or the right – is the way the club-head faces on impact with the ball. When the club-head is open (or angled back) the ball will travel off in a straight line and then veer to the right. This is known as a slice-spin shot. When the club-head is closed (or angled forward), the opposite will occur, where the ball starts straight and then moves off to the left. This is known as a hook-spin shot.

Images the situation where you are hitting toward a target with what is known as a direct swing path. With the club-head open, the ball will start travelling toward the target, then veer off to the right. Equally, with the club-head closed the ball will start straight then move off to the left.

So how, when you apply spin to the ball, should you play the shot to ensure that when the ball moves to the left or right in flight it will even-

tually return on line with the target? The answer is to send it off in a different direction to begin with, and to do this you need to alter the direction of the swing path.

At this stage you may well feel totally confused but in fact the principle is quite straightforward. To simplify the situation think in terms of three sets of shots. The first is where your swing path is directly towards the target; the second is where your swing path travels from inside the target line to outside; and the third is where your swing path travels from outside the target line to inside.

The effect of an open or closed club-head when playing with a direct swing path has already been discussed. When you change the direction of the swing path similar principles apply.

If you have a swing path that travels from inside to outside the target line, when the club-head is also square to that direction at the point of impact, the ball will travel off to the right in a

LEFT: *In order to apply hook-spin to the ball, moving it from right to left in the air, the swing path must be such as to deliver the club-head to the ball travelling from in to out across the ball-to-target line, with the club-face closed from that swing path.*

Side-spin is created by a combination of club-head angle and swing path direction. An in-to-out swing path with a closed club-head produces a 'draw' (A) or, in extreme cases, a 'hook' (B). An out-to-in swing path with an open club-head produces a 'fade' (D) or, in extreme cases a 'slice' (C). A direct swing path with a square club-head produces a straight shot (F), with the club-head open it produces a slight 'fade' (E) and with the club-head closed a 'draw' (G).

straight line and not deviate. Where the club-head is open from that swing path on impact, the ball will travel off to the right then veer even further to the right. With the club-head closed, it will move off to the right then veer back to the left.

If your swing-path is from outside the target line to inside it, when the club-head is square to that swing path at the point of impact, the ball will travel off to the left in a straight line and keep going. Where the club-head is open on impact, the ball will travel off to the left then curve back to the right. With the club-head closed on impact, the ball will go off to the left and then veer sharply away even further left.

How far off target to the right or the left you play the shot will depend on how much you alter your swing path – from inside to outside or vice-versa. Likewise, the amount the ball deviates when in flight will depend on how much you angle the club-head open or closed from the chosen swing path.

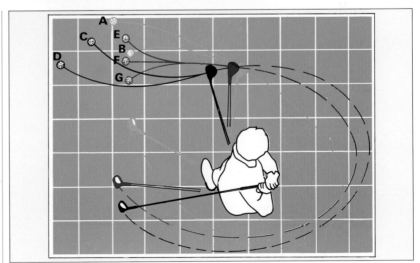

Thus far the principles of side-spin have been discussed – what actually needs to happen to the ball to send it in different directions. Having understood how side-spin works, you will need to learn how to apply it.

APPLYING SLICE-SPIN

Here you need to select the less lofted clubs in the set. The driver is suitable, as is the 3 wood and probably any iron up to 5. The difference in the stance for a hook-spin and a slice-spin shot is that with the latter you do need to alter the complete stance.

The stance for a slice-spin shot should be open from the target line, with feet and hips turned to the left along with the shoulders. Make sure that the ball is further forward in the stance than usual and keep the club-head facing the target, which means it will appear open from the swing path you require for the shot.

When you swing back, you will find that there is nowhere near the same amount of turn in the shoulders and that your swing plane is much more upright, enabling the club to travel down and through the ball from the outside of the target line to the inside.

Again you must make sure that the club-head makes contact with the ball as it crosses the target line. Because the club-head is open on impact with the ball, it will create a clockwise rotation that will eventually take the ball off to the right of its original direction.

One way of getting past an obstacle such as this tree (right) is to slice around it. This can be done by using a straight-faced club and swinging with an upright swing place so that the swing path is from out to in. The blade is kept open long into the follow-through (far right).

RIGHT: *It takes a great deal of courage, once you have aimed sufficiently right of an obstacle such as these trees, to then create an in-to-out swing path, for the impression gained is that the ball will be sent even further to the right than is required. However, with skill and practice, the club-face will be closed from the swing path at the point of impact, causing the ball to turn quite violently in the air from right to left (far right).*

APPLYING HOOK-SPIN

You need to select a lofted club when attempting to play with hook-spin, keeping your left hand forward in the stance and angling the club back slightly. The ball should be positioned further back in the stance than normal for the club you are using.

You may be tempted to close the stance somewhat, by turning your body across the target line. However, the only part of your body that should be turned in to the right is your shoulders, since the line of your shoulders – as with the normal direct line of the swing – will determine the line your swing-path takes. In the case of hook-spin, this needs to be inside to outside across the target line. How far to the right you need to close your shoulders will depend on how far off line you want to send the ball initially.

You will find from this stance and adjusted posture that the swing plane gets shallower and your body turns much more. When you bring the club down, this helps to ensure that it crosses the target line as the ball is struck.

Because the club-head is closed when it makes contact, this will create an anti-clockwise rotation of the ball that will eventually take it off to the left of the original direction of the shot. The more spin you want to put on the ball, the more you need to exaggerate the changes you make to the normal techniques.

Happily not all shots have to be trick ones – and the best shot of all is the one truly struck with the only spin involved being back-spin, to stop the ball dead on the green.

WHEN TO USE SPIN

The obvious advantage to be gained by using spin is when you need to bend the ball around an obstacle on the course that stands between you and the target. However, many professionals also use spin to advantage in normal shots because they feel they have a greater control over the ball and know that it can only travel in a specific direction, depending on the type of spin they apply. This is not a use recommended for the beginner.

Hook-spin is useful when there are problems on the right-hand side of the fairway. Possibly it is an awkward tree, which you are unable to lift the ball over, or maybe a hazard such as water, a bunker or an 'out of bounds' area. Those players confident of gaining sufficient length and height with the ball to surmount such hazards may go for the straight shot. The choice facing the less committed player is either to play safe by hitting away from the trouble or to use spin to play around it.

Slice-spin can be of particular advantage once you have understood its effects and mastered the control of it. Whereas a straight shot, slightly mishit, could end up to the left or right of the target, with slice-spin you know that the ball will move to the right and should be able to judge how far it will do so.

The higher up the ball's surface your club makes contact, in other words the closer to its horizontal circumference, the more side-spin you can put on it. This means that you can use the longer, less lofted clubs when playing with slice-spin, which has the added advantage of giving you more length in the shot. This is particularly useful when you have an obstacle fairly close in front but want to play the ball as far past it as possible.

Where you need to control the length of such a shot, you can still use the less lofted clubs in order to gain side-spin. But here you will need to hold the club lower down the handle and not swing back so far.

With the more lofted clubs which you would in normal circumstances use for these distances, you will put back-spin on the ball and the effect of this will be to eliminate any side-spin. Thus the ball will carry straight on in the direction of the swing path, making no side turn at all.

Where the average golfer would have to be content with just chipping clear of trouble, one with sufficient skill who can turn the ball in the air may save a stroke by sending the ball all the way to the green.

Although you may feel that turning the club at address is insufficient, this sequence shows the effect at the top of the back swing. When the club-face lies almost horizontal and is 'closed' (top left), on its return to the ball it will impart spin that will turn the ball to the left.

TOP RIGHT: When the toe of the club points directly to the ground once the head returns to the ball it will be 'open' from the target line and the ball will turn to the right.

RIGHT: To emphasize the point, compare these with the perfect 'square' position.

When only a very mild form of spin is required for the shot, there is no need to alter the swing path. By turning the club in the grip slightly outward (far left) or inward (left), as the case may be, the ball will turn gently in the air in that direction.

USING GENTLE SPIN

There will be occasions where you will not necessarily need to apply a full-bodied spin but simply want to vary the flight of the ball slightly to avoid a possible problem like, for example, over-hanging branches on the side of the fairway. In this situation you should still apply some spin – either hook or slice – to the ball, but you do not need to alter the swing for the shot.

The adjustments needed for the shot are very simple. For a slight hook-spin you have to move your stance fractionally to the right, closing it slightly to the target line, and closing the face of the club a little. For a slight slice-spin, all that is required to open the club-face a fraction while turning your stance just off to the left of the target line. The important point to bear in mind with both gentle hooks and slices is that your swing path for both types of shot is only off-line through the mildest of adjustments in your stance. There is a temptation to exaggerate which you must resist.

Having understood the method used to apply a gentle amount of spin, you obviously need to know when to use it. You may be concerned that a particular hazard, although not directly in line with the target, is naggingly close to it and

you want to make sure that you do not land in it if your shot is slightly off target. In such a situation, by putting just a little spin on the ball – hook if the obstacle is on the left and slice if it is on the right – you will avoid trouble.

You can also use gentle side-spin to counteract the effect of cross winds, since this enables the ball to hold a reasonably straight course as the spin works against the opposing wind. In such a situation, where the wind is blowing from left to right, you need to apply slight hook-spin, while if it is blowing from right to left you should neutralise this by playing with a bit of slice-spin. Depending on the strength of the wind, the ball is likely to be blown off line altogether unless you take precautions, and this is particularly the case with a lofted club where the height gained makes the ball become vulnerable.

There is always a tendency when opening or closing the face of the club-head to alter the swing plane in the same direction. This happens if you use your forearms to turn the club-head rather than adjusting the club with your hands. You should turn the club-face in or out, as the case may be, resting it on the turn, and *then* take up your grip while ensuring the blade remains crooked.

BAD WEATHER TECHNIQUE

As if the techniques of golf and the design of the course do not provide a great enough challenge to the player, very often the weather does its best to test one ability even further. Wind and rain are the two most obvious enemies and either can create havoc with your game if you are not able to make the necessary adjustments and treat each with respect.

Learning to cope with the adverse conditions such elements can provide is important, since there is nothing worse than for morale to be sapped and your game to collapse. Inevitably you will drop strokes. You would not be human if you did not. But as long as you can keep these to a minimum and learn to accept this, and are equipped mentally and physically for the struggle, you should be able to keep your spirits up and your game going.

PLAYING IN THE RAIN

Obviously there are limits as to how bad the conditions must be before it becomes impossible to play on. There is no way you can play a ball through great pools of water, for example. If you do find yourself in one, then you are allowed to take relief, according to the rules.

Equally, on the greens you are not expected to putt through a lake. In this situation you can move your ball to a spot that offers a dry passage through to the hole, provided this is a similar distance from the hole as before.

It hardly needs stating that you will get a much poorer contact between a wet club-head and a wet ball than you will with a dry one. While you can keep the club-head dry by wiping it with a towel before you use it, you are not allowed to keep wiping the ball. The only time this is permitted is when you are starting each hole. After drying it before a tee shot, you cannot do so again until you are on the green.

The moral behind this, therefore, is to keep the ball in the air as much as possible. This means using a more lofted club than you would normally use in dry conditions. Because of this, you will have to sacrifice length and therefore maybe a stroke at the longer holes.

This is going to prove a lot less expensive, however, over the course of a round than attempting longer shots that run and run, allowing the ball to get wetter and muddier. Another significant point to bear in mind is that with the straighter-faced clubs the ball is more likely to skid off when the club-head is wet.

One small bonus when it is wet, however, is that the greens become softer and therefore tend to hold the ball back more. This allows you to play much stronger shots to the green and be more positive with your putting, safe in the knowledge that the ball is unlikely to run on far, if at all.

Having considered the problems posed for the clubs and the ball, what about the player? If the lower standard of golf is not enough to try your patience and dampen your spirits, then the feeling of being soaked through to the skin certainly will. Be prepared when you go out on the course, particularly if rain is forecast. In the two or three hours you are likely to be playing the round, the weather can change dramatically and it does not take long for rain to soak your clothes.

Take a waterproof suit with you and a change of glove, since you will make stroke play even harder if your grip keeps slipping on the greasy handle. Wear good spiked shoes to give you the best possible grip with your feet and cap to protect your head. Keep several towels and dry cloths in your golf bag, as well, so that you can wipe the clubs each time you use them. Headcovers will help protect your clubs from the rain while they are kept in the bag.

Playing in the rain can be a thoroughly demoralizing experience, but even top professionals like Severiano Ballesteros have to grin and bear it. If you have a caddy it is a good idea to take advantage of whatever shelter you can get when lining up a shot.

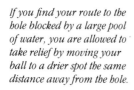

If you find your route to the hole blocked by a large pool of water, you are allowed to take relief by moving your ball to a drier spot the same distance away from the hole.

PLAYING IN THE WIND

However hard and accurately you strike the ball, the presence of a strong wind is bound to affect its flight. Wind is a constant problem on the golf course, particularly on the coastal links where you can always expect some breeze off the sea.

A further problem on such courses is that there is normally little shelter in the way of trees or rising ground. Even on inland courses, where there is this type of shelter, once the ball is in the air the wind will catch it and blow it about. In addition, there is still the chance that the wind will be blowing up or down the fairway, creating a tunnel effect.

Playing in windy conditions is a skill that even a moderate golfer can master. With this skill much advantage can be gained over generally better players who find themselves struggling to control the ball. It is basically a question of recognising the strengths and weaknesses in your own game and playing to them.

In most cases there will be a choice – to take advantage of the prevailing conditions and play with the wind or to go on the attack and try playing against it in the hope of neutralising its effect on the particular shot. There is no easy answer as to which method will work best. Only experience and an understanding of your own capabilities will teach you when to play defensively and when to play aggressively.

FOLLOWING WIND

You get an obvious feeling of cooperation when the wind is blowing from directly behind you, since it will help you carry the ball further than you would normally be able to hit it. However, this advantage can only be obtained by lofting the shot. The higher you can send the ball, the more help the wind can give, so use a club with more loft than you would normally choose.

Before you rush to enlist the help of the wind, bear in mind how much further the ball is likely to travel and where you hope it will land. The extra length you gain with the help of the wind may now put you in range of hazards that you would normally not have reached. There is little point in going for those extra yards if this means winding up in a stream or bunker – or even running off a fairway where it bends to the left or right in a dogleg. If you are concerned that the extra distance could put you in trouble then use a shorter club.

A following wind can pose special problems at short holes. Bearing in mind the siting of bunkers to trap the unwary, with the wind increasing the distance of your shot, the margin of error when aiming onto the green is greatly reduced. A further difficulty you may experience is trying to control the ball when it lands and preventing it from racing right across the green. One way of restricting the run of the ball after it has landed is to play the ball higher and softer. Because it will then come down at a steeper angle and at less pace, it should not run on too far. The loftier the club, the greater help it will be, as will the use of a slightly raised tee peg. In any case, even if the ball does run to the back end of the green, the longer putt will be a lot easier and safer to play than trying to hit a plugged ball out of the sand. The answer is not to be too ambitious and, when in doubt, play safe.

So far only the benefits of a following wind have been discussed and, of course, these should be used to your advantage as much and as often as possible. But this type of wind does have its disadvantages, too. And these are no more clearly demonstrated than when playing a short shot to the green. Here ball control is all important and the effect of the following wind works completely against this.

The real trouble with the following wind, as already mentioned, is that it has a habit of neutralising any back-spin you put on the ball, which is the essential ingredient of a short shot because it enables the ball to stop virtually dead on the green. The way to get around this dilemma is to use a very lofted club, such as a pitching wedge, or even, where there is sufficient grass underneath, a sand iron. By using one of these clubs you can get maximum height with minimum pace on the ball and increase the chances of the ball stopping soon after landing.

Remember too, the other methods already discussed for increasing the loft of a shot. These include having the ball fairly forward in the stance so that your shoulders are lined up slightly more open and your club swings down and through from outside to inside the line of the shot.

HEAD WIND

This type of wind makes life very difficult for the golfer. The natural reaction is to force the ball that much harder to counteract the effect of the wind blowing against the flight. Of course this approach is fraught with dangers, since by trying to hit harder you are likely to introduce or exaggerate faults in the swing.

Some people think that by keeping the ball on a lower trajectory this will help minimise the effect of the wind. As a result, they turn the club-face in at the address to reduce its loft. But by reducing the loft, you risk ballooning the shot.

There is no simple solution to this problem. What you must resign yourself to is the fact that length will be lost in the wind and you must be

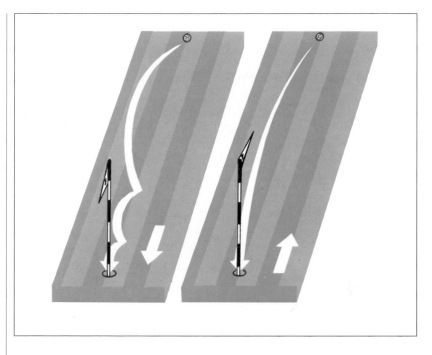

prepared to drop the odd stroke at the longer holes. As a general guide, particularly when playing off the tee, aim to get a bit of hook-spin on the ball, since this will help it to run on further after landing. This entails having the ball further back when you take up your stance, with your shoulders lining up fractionally closed to the line of the shot.

What you must avoid at all costs is putting any slice-spin on the ball, which will happen if the ball is too far forward in the stance. If you do, you will sacrifice even more length in the shot. Equally avoid putting any back-spin on the ball. Since the rotation of the ball is with the wind, the net effect will be to hold the ball up longer and again valuable distance will be lost. To play safe, it may be worth dropping your hands down the club-handle fractionally to shorten the swing. The effect of this is to eliminate wrist activity and give greater control.

A strong head wind can work in your favour at some short holes or when you are playing a short shot to the green. In either case, the wind will hold the ball up and add to the effect of any back-spin by preventing the ball from running forward after it has landed on the green.

With your tee shot to the shorter holes you can safely use a club with a lot less loft than you

The consolation of playing a shot into the wind is the knowledge that all short iron shots will stop immediately on landing. This means that the ball can be hit firmly right up to the flag (above).

When playing with a following wind, you should aim to land the ball short of the target so that it may run on up to the flag (above left).

would normally and aim for the green, confident in the knowledge that the head wind will hold the ball and cause it to descend sharply. The only danger you face is that should the ball fall short of the target and drop into a bunker, it will do so steeply and present you with additional problems if it plugs in the sand.

Where you are faced with a short shot to the green, you can afford to play a firm stroke and use a short swing. It is best to move your grip down the handle and keep the ball positioned reasonably well back in the stance. In this way you should be able to guarantee good control, plenty of loft and back-spin which, helped by the direction of the wind, will stop the ball on landing.

It could be, on a long hole, that you need to gain maximum distance from your second shot. In this situation you can use one of the fairway woods and swing with your grip moved slightly down the handle.

CROSS WIND

The problem with cross winds is not so much one of length, but rather direction. If you play a normal straight shot with little or no spin, the wind is bound to move the ball off line to the left or right, depending on where it is blowing from.

With the wind coming from the left, you can expect the ball to be blown to the right of the intended line of the shot. Moreover, what is worse is that a strong cross wind, which is blowing against your back, tends to push your body forward and too much over the ball. From this position you are quite likely to slice the shot, thus exaggerating the problem. One way to counteract this is to use a loftier club and put some hook-spin on the ball. This helps to keep the ball pulling to the left against the wind and thus, hopefully, maintain a direct course to the target. This is fine when you are playing with an iron – and it is to a degree possible with the more lofted woods, but you should not attempt to hook the ball with a driver, since this club as too little loft.

The alternative to hook-spin – and once you may decide it is easier to adopt in all situations of this kind – is to aim the ball fractionally off to the left and leave the wind to bring it back on line

with the target. How far off line you decide to aim will depend on how strong the wind is at the time and how much deviation it is likely to cause.

When the wind blows the other way – from the right and into the player – there are generally fewer problems to contend with. This is particularly true with the longer shots, where by aiming off to the right of the target you can afford to play a full-blooded shot and leave the wind to push it back on line.

Life on the golf course, however, is not so easy when you are playing onto the green, since it is hard to control the ball in a right to left wind and prevent it from running on too far. In this situation there are two fairly simple choices. You can play short of the green to cut down the margin of error and leave yourself a chip shot to the hole.

Alternatively, you can aim for the front of the green, accepting the fact that the ball will almost certainly run on and end up at the back, possibly leaving you with a longish putt back to the hole. In either case, you will need to adjust your aim and play to the right of your target – that is, into the wind.

If you feel sufficiently confident to play the shot with some hook-spin and so gain extra distance, then use a club with slightly more loft and take up your stance with the ball positioned further back than normal. By playing the shot out into the wind, and adding your hook technique, the ball should then fly back in a big curve onto its course with the help of the spin.

Those players who can control slice-spin have the option of using it here and can aim directly at the target with a less lofted club.

WINDY GREENS

Putting in windy conditions can pose problems. Depending on the length of the shot, some adjustment to the line you take should be made. Where there is a slope and the wind is blowing down it, you need to increase the amount of borrow. Conversely, with the wind against the slope, you can afford to reduce it.

A head wind on the green should cause no trouble and, in fact, can be of definite help since it allows you to play a much firmer, more positive

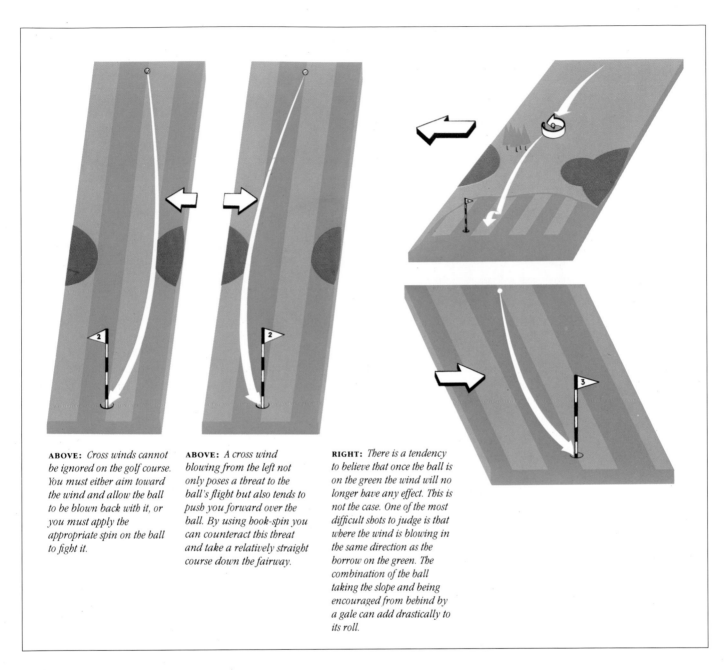

ABOVE: *Cross winds cannot be ignored on the golf course. You must either aim toward the wind and allow the ball to be blown back with it, or you must apply the appropriate spin on the ball to fight it.*

ABOVE: *A cross wind blowing from the left not only poses a threat to the ball's flight but also tends to push you forward over the ball. By using hook-spin you can counteract this threat and take a relatively straight course down the fairway.*

RIGHT: *There is a tendency to believe that once the ball is on the green the wind will no longer have any effect. This is not the case. One of the most difficult shots to judge is that where the wind is blowing in the same direction as the borrow on the green. The combination of the ball taking the slope and being encouraged from behind by a gale can add drastically to its roll.*

shot to the hole. The worst situation is where you are putting down a slope and the wind is blowing from behind you. Then you have to judge the pace of the ball very carefully or you will find it racing away past the hole to the other side of the green.

Extra care should be taken when playing short shots onto the green. Although you may not be sending the ball very far, thus giving the wind less time to affect its line, the height of the shot can make the ball vulnerable. Thus you should avoid, as far as possible, floating the ball too much in the air.

Depending on the direction of the wind, the ball may pull up more quickly when the wind is against you. Equally it will run on more with the wind behind. It may in some situations be better to play a shorter chip shot and let the ball run toward the hole, rather than attempt to pitch it right up to the hole and misjudge the reaction of the wind.

COMMON FAULTS

Golf shots fly off-line for many reasons. The fault may be in your own hands, your stance, your head position, swing, aim or balance. To identify typical faults you must first understand the concepts of target line and swing line. The target line runs from the ball to the target. That is the line which you take when lining up your shot. The swing line is the actual line taken by the club-head as it goes from the backswing down into the ball and through to your finish.

If the club-head goes back and then through on the same line, then it is in plane. If, however, from the top of the backswing you are in an up-right position and at the finish of the shot you are in a flat position then you will have swung out of plane, on an out-to-in swing line. The opposite occurs when your hands at the top of the back-swing are in a flat position and at the finish of the

The golfing terms for the direction of shot.

follow-through have moved into an upright posi-tion – then you have swung from in-to-out.

CAUSES OF BAD SHOTS

The causes of bad shots are easiest explained in terms of table tennis. In this game slices and spins are exaggerated and intentional, and the effects easier to see than in golf.

THE SLICE

The slice is a shot where the ball sets off to the left of the target line (still in terms of right-handed players) and swerves in the air to finish right off the target line. The ball has the same flight as the back-spin shot in table tennis. To play this shot the table tennis bat is held open to the target line and the swing line is from out-to-in and the bat cuts across the target line under the ball. The ball swerves from left to right.

THE PULL

The pull shot goes straight to the left of your in-tended target line without any swerve. In table tennis the bat takes an out-to-in swing, coming across the target line, but with the face of the bat square to the actual swing line. The ball would miss the table on the left.

THE PUSH

The push shot sends the golf ball straight to the right of the target line. Its equivalent table tennis shot also flies straight and misses the table on the right. It is effected by an in-to-out swing path with the bat face square to the swing line.

THE HOOK

The flight of a hooked ball starts to the right of the target line and swings in the air to finish left of the target line. In table tennis, its nearest equivalent is the smash, which has an in-to-out swing with the bat face closed to the target line, causing top-spin.

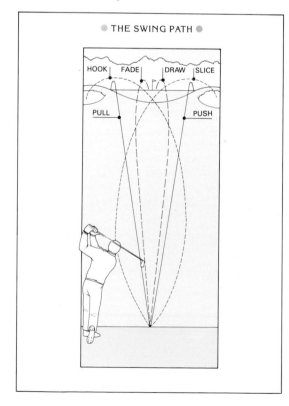

● THE SWING PATH ●

HOOK | FADE | DRAW | SLICE

PULL | PUSH

ABOVE: *(1) The slice is the same as the back-spin shot in table tennis. The feet are open, aiming left of the target line, with the bat also lying open.*

(2) The hands are in an open position at the top of the backswing.

(3) To reach the top of the follow-through, the table tennis bat cuts across the target line, putting back-spin on the ball.

ABOVE: *The hook is closest to the table tennis smash. The feet are closed to the target line (pointing to the right).*

ABOVE: *At the top of the backswing, the bat is on the inside of the target line.*

ABOVE: *To reach the top of the follow-through, the bat travels from the inside, at the top of the backswing, to the outside at the top of the follow-through. The table tennis bat turns over, putting top-spin or over-spin on the ball. The flight of the ball is from right to left.*

You must analyse your own game to find any faults with your aim, grip, stance, the position of the ball or your swing to discover the cause of any of your own wayward shots. Listed below are some ideas to help diagnose the possible cause of the trouble.

You might *slice* shots because:

● In your aim the club blade is open to the target.

● Your grip is too weak.

● Your feet or body are lined up left of the target in the stance.

● In your swing, you open the club-face at the start of the backswing.

● Your wrists cup at the top of the backswing, which also causes an open face.

● You are starting the downswing with the right shoulder coming out towards the ball, causing an out-to-in swing.

TOP: *At the top of the backswing, the back of the left hand and wrist must be level. This ensures that the club-head is square to the plane.*

FAR LEFT: *If your grip is too weak, the club-face will open on impact, causing the ball to slice.*

ABOVE AND LEFT: *If the wrists are cupped at the top of the backswing, the club-face will be open.*

You might *pull* shots because:

● In your aim, the club-face is pointing left of the target.

● In your stance and position in relation to the ball, your body alignment is forcing you to the left and the ball is too far forward.

● In the swing you are not transferring your weight properly in the follow-through, but continuing to support your body weight on your right foot.

You might *push* your shots because:

● In your stance and ball position, the body alignment is forcing you to the right, with the ball too far back from the centre line between your feet.

● In your swing, your body weight is being transferred too early onto your left leg.

You might *hook* shots because:

● In your aim, the blade of the club is closed to the target.

● Your grip is too strong.

● In the stance and ball position your feet and body are facing to the right of the target.

● In your swing you are closing the club-face at the start of the backswing.

● Your wrists are bowed at the top of the backswing, which closes the club-face.

TOP: *If you pull your shots consistently to the left, it could be that your club-head is pointing to the left of the target at the address position.*

CENTRE LEFT: *Make sure that your wrists are not bowed at the top of the backswing, which will tend to make you hook.*

CENTRE: *If you push your shots consistently to the right, your club-face may be pointing to the right of the target.*

FAR LEFT: *Make sure that your grip is not too strong: this will also make you hook the ball.*

LEFT: *If you close the club-face at the start of the swing, you will hook.*

INDEX

References in italics refer to illustration captions.

ACKNOWLEDGEMENTS

Thanks to La Manga Club, Costa Calida, Spain, for use of their facilities and location photography. Photographs: **Ian Howes** 10, 11, 12, 13, 14, 15, 17, 18, 19, 20, 21, 22, 23, 24, 25, 26, 27, 76, 77, 78, 79, 80, 81, 82, 83, 84, 85, 86, 87, 88, 89, 90, 91, 92, 93, 95, 98, 99, 100, 101, 102, 103, 119, 120, 121, 124, 125, 126, 127, 128, 129, 130, 133, 136, 137, 139, 140. **E D Lacy** 132. **Brent Moore** 117, 123, 132. **David Muscroft** 16. **Phil Sheldon** 27, 28, 29, 30, 31, 32, 34, 35, 36, 37, 38, 39, 40, 41, 42, 43, 44, 46, 47, 48, 49, 50, 52, 53, 54, 55, 56, 57, 58, 59, 60, 61, 62, 63, 64, 65, 66, 69, 70, 72, 73, 85, 115, 116, 117.

Illustration: **Mick Hill** 94, 96, 123, 134, 135. **Rob Schone** 76, 138.